Country Style
Quilting

Country Style Quilting

Lynette Anderson

David and Charles

www.stitchcraftcreate.co.uk

Contents

For Elsie,

*my beautiful granddaughter, who I can't wait to teach to
stitch just as my grandmother taught me.*

Introduction

The happy song that the little birds in this world sing for us never ceases to make me smile and I hope that the birds featured in some of these projects make you feel happy too. The little bird reminds me of all that is good in the world and he features in many of my designs. I can almost draw him with my eyes closed! From big quilts to the small projects, I have had such fun drawing and stitching them for you to enjoy. A big thank you is due to my wonderful team of stitching helpers. My absolute favourite is the heirloom 'quilt of the future', the Hexie Heirloom Quilt, made from the hundreds of appliqué birds that I have made during my Apliquick™ tool demonstrations in classes around the world. This quilt has special memories for me, and my husband and I are looking forward to having it on our bed one day. I hope making the projects in this book will bring special memories to you, too.

Projects

There are fourteen lovely projects in this book for you to make, including bed quilts, throws, cushions, wall hangings, sewing accessories and table linen. The projects are my usual mix of techniques, including patchwork, appliqué, hand embroidery and machine quilting, and are suitable for a wide range of abilities. Do read all the project instructions before you start a project, to familiarize yourself with what is required. The projects use a ¼in (6mm) seam allowance, unless otherwise stated. The Valdani threads that I have chosen to use for many of the projects are hand dyed. I love the subtle shading and variegation of colour throughout the skein, which lends itself to my designs superbly. DMC alternatives are provided for you, if required, in the Materials & Equipment section.

Measurements

Imperial and metric measurements have been given in the book, with metric in brackets (parenthesis). The projects were made using Imperial measurements, so the best results will be obtained using this system.

Fabrics

At the start of each project there is a 'You Will Need' list that describes the fabrics needed and the quantity. I frequently use my own fabrics for a project, and these choices are often suggested in the project text, but you can, of course, use others if you prefer. The Daisy Chain Cottages Quilt was based on a specific fabric range, so a more detailed list of the fabric I used is given for that quilt. Fabric quantities are based on a 42in (107cm) width of fabric, unless otherwise stated.

Diagrams

Drawings have been given to illustrate the stepped text where necessary. These are not to scale but are just intended to support the text

Basic Techniques

All of the projects have the instructions, diagrams and photographs you need to make them successfully. There are a few techniques that are common to many of the projects and these are given in a section at the back of the book. It is a good idea to read through this section before you start any project.

Appliqué and embroidery are favourite techniques of mine, especially traditional needle-turn appliqué. The projects can use either needle-turn appliqué or fusible web appliqué. Both methods are described in detail in the Basic Techniques section. Just remember that needle-turn appliqué requires a small seam allowance around each motif, usually ⅛in–¼in (3mm–6mm). Fusible web appliqué does not need a seam allowance because the edges are normally oversewn in some way, usually with blanket stitch. If using the templates for fusible web appliqué you will need to reverse (flip) them before use.

Templates

One of my favourite parts of quilting is the appliqué and stitchery, so most of the projects use templates. These have been provided full size in the Templates section at the back of the book.

I have had fun using fabrics that I have designed for the projects in this book, and it's wonderful to see how nicely the different collections have mixed together to create a scrappy look for some of the projects. I hope you have fun creating some fabulous projects for yourself, your family and your friends.

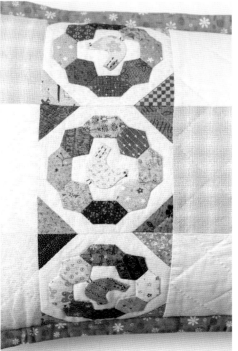

Lynette x.*

Hexi Birds

The little appliqué birds in this quilt were all made whilst demonstrating the Apliquick™ tools at various workshops around the globe. I wanted to keep the little birds to remind me of the many lovely people that I met on my journeys and came up with the idea of combining them in a wonderful scrappy-looking quilt. I have given a suggestion for the fabric requirements but feel free to add a larger mixture of fabrics to your quilt – the more the merrier! The quilt does take some time to make but the result is an heirloom piece that I'm sure you and your family will be delighted with for decades to come.

The smaller project in this chapter is a lovely pillowcase using only three of the bird blocks. It matches the quilt and makes a gorgeous addition to any bed. It is designed to fit a standard bed pillow.

Hexi Heirloom Quilt

You will need…

❀ Ten assorted cream-on-cream prints (I used some yarn-dyed fabrics to add texture), ½yd (0.5m) of each

❀ Fifty assorted coordinating prints for elongated hexagons, hexagons and birds, 2½in (6.4cm) x width of fabric of each

❀ Thirty-eight assorted coordinating prints for corner squares 2in (5cm) x width of fabric of each

❀ 784 pre-cut paper hexagons with ⅝in (1.6cm) sides (see Tip below)

❀ 784 pre-cut paper elongated hexagons with ⅝in (1.6cm) and ⅞in (2.2cm) sides (see Tip)

❀ Fusible water-soluble appliqué paper (optional)

❀ Fabric glue pen (such as Sewline, Bohin or Fons & Porter)

❀ Stranded embroidery cotton (floss): Cosmo #895 charcoal (or DMC #844)

❀ Wadding (batting) about 78in (198cm) square

❀ Backing fabric 78in (198cm) square

❀ Binding fabric (blue floral) ½yd (0.5m)

Finished size
70in (178cm) square approx.
Use ¼in (6mm) seams unless otherwise stated

Tip

When using needle-turn appliqué, particularly for small shapes, Apliquick™ tools are extremely useful. The fabric is fused to a fusible water-soluble appliqué paper template and the tools are then used to hold the appliqué shape and turn the seam allowance over easily, keeping it in place with a stroke of fabric glue. In the normal method of just using pre-cut paper shapes, I find that when you remove the pre-cut papers the edge of the fabric shape gets distorted, which is frustrating. The appliqué paper doesn't need to be removed – it softens as you handle it and then disintegrates when the project is washed later. You can buy pre-cut hexagons and elongated hexagons at: www.littlestore.com.au (and other online stores). Alternatively, use the templates provided in the Templates section. For a quicker result, download the pages of hexagons, elongated hexagons and bird appliqué templates supplied at www.stitchcraftcreate.com, and print out the pages directly onto fusible water-soluble appliqué paper (on an ink-jet printer only).

−✕−✕− ✕−✕− ✕− ✕−✕−✕− ✕−✕−✕−✕−✕−✕−✕

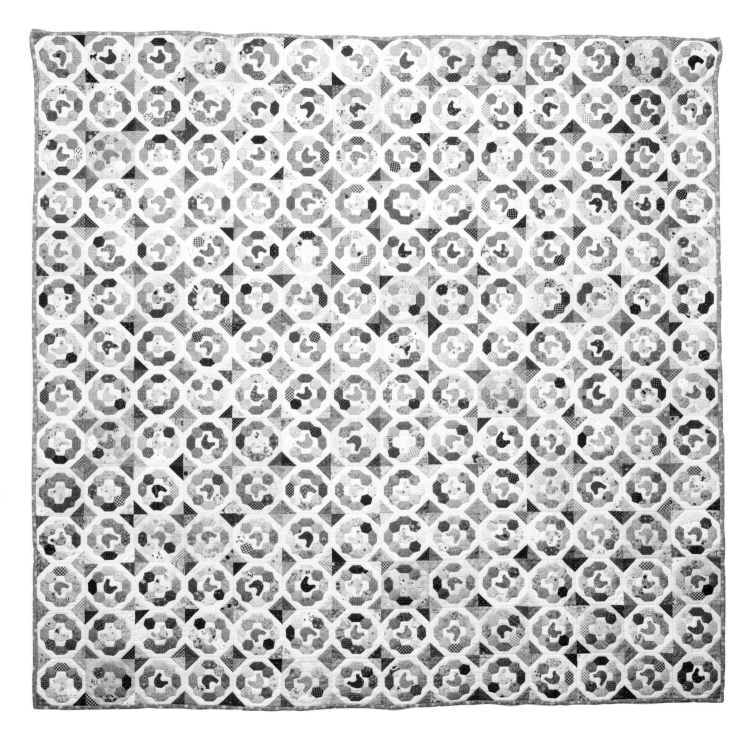

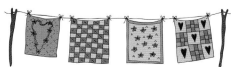

Cutting out

1 From each of the ten assorted cream-on-cream prints cut twenty 5½in (14cm) squares, for a total of 200 squares. You will need 196. The spares can be used for the pillow project.

2 From each of the thirty-eight assorted coordinating prints cut twenty-one 2in (5cm) squares (for corner triangles), for a total of 798 squares. The spares can be used for the pillow project.

3 From the binding fabric cut eight strips each 2¼in (5.7cm) x width of fabric.

Making the bird blocks

4 Take the 2in (5cm) fabric squares (for the corner triangles) and on the wrong side draw a line diagonally across each square using a suitable fabric marker (I prefer a 2B pencil). This will be your stitching line (Fig 1).

5 Choosing cream-on-cream print 5½in (14cm) squares at random, place a 2in (5cm) square, right sides together, with a larger square. Stitch on the drawn line (Fig 2A). Trim excess fabric away (Fig 2B). Press the triangle open (Fig 2C).

6 Add a small square to all corners of the larger square in the same way (Fig 3). Check the sewn block is 5½in (14cm) square. Sew the rest of the blocks in the same way, for a total of 196 blocks.

Fig 1

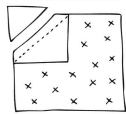

Draw a diagonal line on the wrong side of a 2in (5cm) square

Fig 2 A Stitch on drawn line **B** Trim off excess fabric

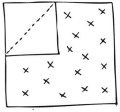

C

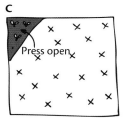

Press open

Fig 3

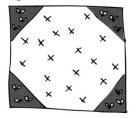

—✕—✕—✕—✕—✕—✕—✕—✕—✕—✕—✕—✕—✕—✕—✕—

Paper piecing the hexagons

7 Using the thirty-eight assorted coordinating prints, prepare the fabric hexagons and the elongated hexagons using an English paper piecing technique (see Basic Techniques: English Paper Piecing). If you are using pre-cut paper shapes then use these to cut out your fabric shapes with an extra ¼in (6mm) seam allowance all round. Alternatively, use the paper and fabric templates supplied in the Templates section. You will need a total of 784 paper hexagons and 784 elongated paper hexagons to create the same numbers of fabric shapes.

8 When all of the shapes are prepared, sew four hexagons and four elongated hexagons together in a ring, alternating the shapes as shown in Fig 4. Repeat to create 196 rings.

Fig 4

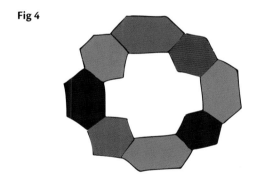

9 Take a ring, place it in the centre of a block and appliqué it in place using a blind hem stitch. Press the work. Repeat with all of the blocks.

Adding the birds

10 Using the appliqué template provided, prepare a bird for needle-turn appliqué (see Basic Techniques: Needle-Turn Appliqué). A seam allowance of ⅛in–¼in (3mm–6mm) will be fine. Apply the bird in place in the centre of the hexagon ring (Fig 5). Using two strands of charcoal embroidery cotton (floss), embroider the legs and beak in backstitch and the eye with a French knot. Add two lines of running stitch on the tail. Repeat with all of the blocks, placing the birds at different angles to add interest.

Fig 5

Assembling the quilt

11 When all of the blocks are finished lay them out in fourteen rows, each with fourteen blocks. I made sure that the birds were angled in different directions, to add further interest to the design. Sew the blocks together, row by row, pressing the seams of alternate rows in opposite directions so the rows will nest together neatly. Now sew the rows together, matching the seams neatly. Press these final seams in one direction, or open if you prefer.

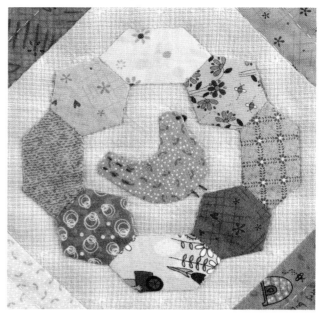

Quilting and finishing

12 Lay the pressed backing right side down, with the smoothed wadding (batting) on top. Lay the quilt top right side up on top, making sure there is wadding and backing showing all round, and then secure the quilt layers together (see Basic Techniques: Making a Quilt Sandwich).

13 Quilt as desired. I had some help creating this quilt in time for this book and my grateful thanks go to Yvonne Dann and friends. Hand quilting was worked by Pam Grant around the hexagon ring, on the inside and outside and also in a diamond pattern within the corner triangles.

14 When all the quilting is finished, tidy all thread ends, square up the quilt and prepare for binding. Join the binding fabric strips together end to end using 45-degree seams. Press the seams open. Fold the strip in half all along the length, wrong sides together and press. Use this strip to bind your quilt – see Basic Techniques: Binding.

Hexi Birds Pillow

You will need…

❋ Fifteen 5½in (14cm) squares of assorted cream-on-cream prints for backgrounds

❋ Twelve 2in (5cm) squares of assorted coordinating fabrics for corner triangles

❋ Assorted 2½in (6.4cm) wide strips of coordinating prints for hexagons and birds

❋ Blue floral print for border, backing and ties ¾yd (0.75m)

❋ Twelve pre-cut paper hexagons with ⅝in (1.6cm) sides (see Tip below)

❋ Twelve pre-cut paper elongated hexagons with ⅝in (1.6cm) and ⅞in (2.2cm) sides (see Tip)

❋ Stranded embroidery cotton (floss): Cosmo #895 charcoal (or DMC #844)

❋ Lightweight wadding (batting) 20in x 30in (50.8cm x 76.2cm)

❋ Muslin/calico 20in x 30in (50.8cm x 76.2cm)

Finished size
17in x 27in (43.2cm x 68.6cm) approx.
Use ¼in (6mm) seams unless otherwise stated

Tip

You will probably have some fabrics left over from the quilt project, which can be used for the pillow. Refer also to the Tip about Apliquick™ tools and the hexagon templates at the start of the quilt instructions.

Making the bird blocks

1 The blocks are made in the same way as for the quilt – see Figs 1–3 in that project if required. Take the 2in (5cm) fabric squares (for the corner triangles) and on the wrong side draw a line diagonally across each square using a suitable fabric marker (I prefer a 2B pencil). This will be your stitching line.

2 Choosing cream-on-cream print 5½in (14cm) squares at random, place one 2in (5cm) square, right sides together, with one of the larger squares. Stitch on the drawn line. Trim excess fabric away. Press the triangle open.

3 Add a small square to all corners of the larger square in the same way. Check the block is 5½in (14cm) square. Sew the other two bird blocks in the same way, for a total of three blocks.

Paper piecing the hexagons

4 The hexagons are pieced in the same way as for the quilt. Using the assorted coordinating prints, prepare the fabric hexagons and the elongated hexagons using an English paper piecing technique (see Basic Techniques: English Paper Piecing). If using pre-cut paper shapes then use these to cut out your fabric shapes with an extra ¼in (6mm) seam allowance all round. Alternatively, use the paper and fabric templates supplied in the Templates section. You will need a total of twelve paper hexagons and twelve elongated paper hexagons to create the fabric shapes.

5 When all of the shapes are prepared, sew four hexagons and four elongated hexagons together in a ring, alternating the shapes. Repeat to create three rings in total.

6 Take a ring and place it in the centre of a block, appliquéing in place using a blind hem stitch. Press the work. Repeat with the other two blocks.

Adding the birds

7 Using the appliqué template provided, prepare a bird for needle-turn appliqué (see Basic Techniques: Needle-Turn Appliqué). A seam allowance of ⅛in–¼in (3mm–6mm) will be fine. Appliqué the bird in the centre of the hexagon ring. Using two strands of charcoal embroidery cotton (floss), embroider the bird's legs and beak in backstitch and the eye with a French knot. Add two lines of running stitch on the tail. Repeat with the other blocks, placing the birds at slightly different angles to add interest.

Piecing the pillow front

8 Take the remaining cream-on-cream squares and the three bird blocks and sew them together into three rows, each with four blocks (Fig 1). For each row, start with a plain square, then a bird block and then three plain squares. Press the seams of the middle row in the opposite direction to the other rows. Sew the rows together, matching seams neatly.

Fig 1

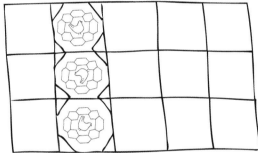

9 From the blue floral fabric cut the following (see Fig 2).

❀ Two strips each 1½in x 25½in (3.8cm x 64.8cm), for the top and bottom borders.

❀ Two strips each 1½in x 17½in (3.8cm x 44.4cm), for the side borders.

❀ Four strips each 1½in x 13½in (3.8cm x 34.3cm), for ties.

❀ One rectangle 17½in x 17in (44.4cm x 43.2cm), for the back of the pillow.

❀ One rectangle 17½in x 15in (44.4cm x 38.1cm), for the back of the pillow.

Fig 2

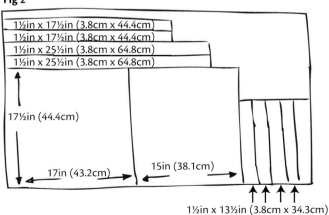

1½in x 17½in (3.8cm x 44.4cm)
1½in x 17½in (3.8cm x 44.4cm)
1½in x 25½in (3.8cm x 64.8cm)
1½in x 25½in (3.8cm x 64.8cm)

17½in (44.4cm)

17in (43.2cm)   15in (38.1cm)

1½in x 13½in (3.8cm x 34.3cm)

10 Sew 1½in x 25½in (3.8cm x 64.8cm) strips to the top and bottom of the pillow (Fig 3A). Press seams outwards. Sew 1½in x 17½in (3.8cm x 44.4cm) strips to the sides (Fig 3B).

Fig 3

A

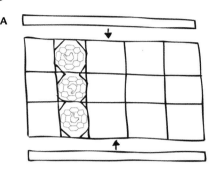

B

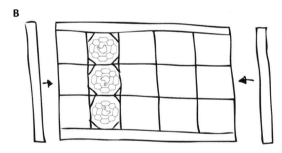

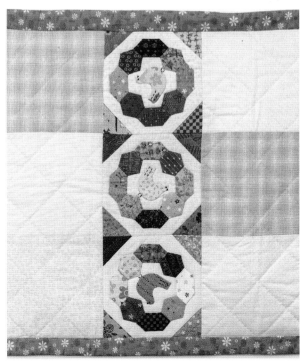

Quilting the front

11 Place the 20in x 30in (50.8cm x 76.2cm) piece of muslin on a flat surface, add the piece of wadding (batting) on top and smooth out. Add the pillow front, right side up, and secure the layers with a method of your choice (see Basic Techniques: Making a Quilt Sandwich). Quilt as desired. I hand quilted around the inside and outside of the hexagon rings. Further machine quilting was added in a diagonal cross-hatch pattern across the plain squares, with lines about 2in (5cm) apart.

Making the pillow back

12 Take the two rectangles of blue floral fabric and on one long edge of each piece turn over a ⅜in (1cm) hem, twice (Fig 4A). Press and then machine stitch in place (Fig 4B).

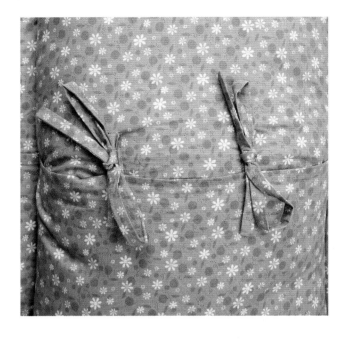

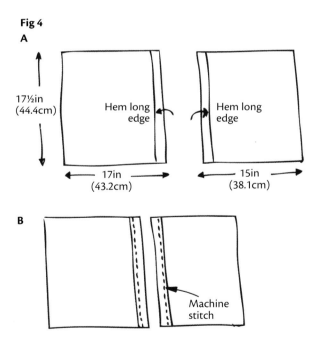

Fig 4

A

17½in (44.4cm)

Hem long edge

Hem long edge

17in (43.2cm)

15in (38.1cm)

B

Machine stitch

Making the ties

13 You need to make four ties for the back of your pillow from the four narrow strips of blue floral fabric cut earlier. Working with one strip at a time, fold the strip in half lengthways, right sides together. Machine stitch across one short end and then down the long edge (Fig 5). Turn the tie through to the right side and press. Turn the raw edge in and slipstitch the opening closed. Make three more ties in the same way.

Fig 5

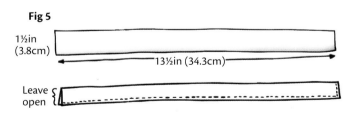

1½in (3.8cm)

13½in (34.3cm)

Leave open

-X-X-X-X-X-X-X-X-X-X-X-X-X-

14 Machine sew the ties to the backing pieces, placing them about 6¼in (15.9cm) in from the short edges, as shown in Fig 6.

16 Turn through to the right side and press. Machine stitch in the seam ditch of the blue floral border all around the pillow (Fig 7). This will create a flat outer edge that gives a nice finish.

Fig 6

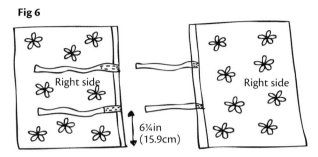

Right side

6¼in
(15.9cm)

Right side

Fig 7

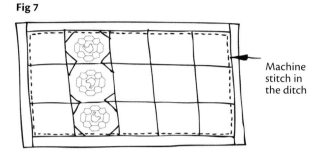

Machine stitch in the ditch

Assembling the pillow

15 Working on a flat surface, place the pillow front right side up. Place the two backing pieces right sides down on top, aligning the outer edges. The backing pieces will overlap in the centre of the pillow. Make sure that the ties are out of the way so they will not get stitched into the side seams. Pin the layers together and then stitch the front and back of the pillow together all around the edge.

Flower Basket

I love to use items intended for one purpose for something entirely different, so imagine my excitement when I was at a friend's wedding and we were served individual portions of steamed rice in little steamer baskets. I was struck with the idea that these baskets, which are easy to find, would make great sewing baskets. You can find them in different sizes in Asian supply stores or kitchen shops.

A scissor holder project is the perfect accompaniment to the sewing box. It's so cute and easy to stitch and would be ideal to give as a gift. It features my little bird and some embroidery, but you could adapt the design if you wish.

Flower Sewing Basket

You will need…

❁ Double steamer basket with lid, 8in (20.5cm) diameter with baskets about 2in (5cm) deep

❁ Cream-on-cream print for stitchery background, 12in (30.5cm) square

❁ Cream feature print for box base lining, one fat quarter

❁ Small purple floral fabric for lining side baskets, 6in (15.2cm) x width of fabric

❁ Scraps of assorted brown prints for appliqué basket, each about 2in (5cm) square

❁ Cotton wadding (batting) for lid and inner basket linings, about 15in x 30in (38cm x 76cm)

❁ Fusible stitchery stabilizer 12in (30.5cm) square (optional)

❁ Valdani stranded embroidery cotton (floss): #P10 antique violet, #JP122 seaside, #078 aged wine, #P5 tarnished gold, #0511 black sea, #0575 crispy leaf (see Materials & Equipment: Threads for DMC alternatives)

❁ Nine paper triangles and one square, for English paper piecing (see Step 2 and Templates section)

❁ Thin card (e.g., cereal packet weight)

❁ Fine-tipped fabric marking pen (removable if you prefer)

❁ Fast-tack craft glue and a glue stick suitable for use on fabric

❁ Template plastic about 9in (23cm) square

❁ Kitchen aluminium foil

❁ Light box or light pad (optional)

Finished size
8in (20.3cm) diameter approx.
Use ¼in (6mm) seams unless otherwise stated

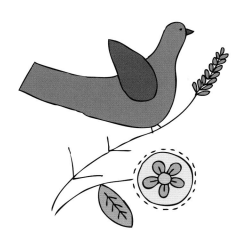

Transferring the stitchery design

1 Copy the stitchery and appliqué template for the basket lid from the Templates section. Using a light source, such as a light box or window, centre the cream-on-cream stitchery background fabric right side up over the pattern and trace the stitchery lines carefully using a fine-tipped fabric pen.

Working the appliqué

2 The basket is made of small triangles and one square, sewn together using traditional English paper piecing. Use the templates provided to cut one square and nine triangles. Templates with seam allowances are given. Tack (baste) the fabric square and triangles around the paper templates (or better still, use a glue stick), as shown in Fig 1. See also Basic Techniques: English Paper Piecing for more information on this technique. Sew the square and triangles together using whip stitches and matching sewing thread, to make the shape shown in Fig 2. Press the work firmly and then remove the paper templates.

3 Using tiny slipstitches and matching thread, appliqué the basket to the background fabric, positioning it as shown on the template.

4 Add the bird appliqué as follows. Using the bird body and wing shapes provided and your favourite method of appliqué, prepare the appliqué shapes. If you plan to use needle-turn appliqué, add ¼in (6mm) seam allowance to the shapes. If using fusible web appliqué, reverse the shapes before using. I made templates for the appliqué shapes from paper and used needle-turn appliqué to sew the bird in place. See Basic Techniques: Appliqué.

Fig 1

Fig 2

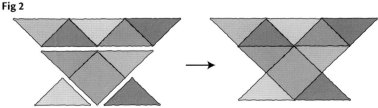

Working the stitchery

5 If you are using an iron-on stitchery stabilizer, fuse it to the back of the fabric before starting the embroidery. Using this will also avoid thread shadows showing on the front of your work. Place the shiny side of the stabilizer on to the wrong side of your fabric and bond it in place with an iron, following the manufacturer's instructions.

6 Use two strands of Valdani embroidery thread. See Basic Techniques: Embroidery Stitches for how to work the stitches and Materials & Equipment: Threads for DMC alternatives. Stitches used are (abbreviations in brackets): backstitch (BS), satin stitch (SS), running stitch (RS), detached lazy daisy (DLD), cross stitch (CS), blanket stitch (BLKS) and French knots (FK). When all embroidery is complete press the work carefully.

Tip For most of my appliqué work I now use Apliquick products, in conjunction with a new appliqué paper that is water soluble and single sided (a brilliant product) – see Basic Techniques: Appliqué for details.

 #P10 Antique violet
Lavender flowers (double row of DLD with FKs along centre)

 #JP12 Seaside
Outer edge of daisy flowers (BLKS)
Dashed circles around flowers (RS)
Markings on bird's tail (RS)

 #078 Aged wine
Petals on inner daisy flower (BS)
Outer circular line (BS)
Crosses on outer border (CS)

 #P5 Tarnished gold
Bird's beak (SS)

 #0511 Black sea
Flower centres (BS circle with four FKs)
Bird eye (FK)
Bird legs (BS)

 #0575 Crispy leaf
Flower stems and leaves (BS)

−X−X−X−X−X−X−X−X−X−X−X−X−X−X−X

Preparing the steamer

7 Cut off the little handle on the lid of the steamer basket (use some old scissors as the basket is tough). Measure the inside diameter of the steamer basket lid – mine was about 8in (20.5cm) – and make a template this size from template plastic.

8 Centre the circle template over the wrong side of the stitchery/appliqué. Draw a line around the template and then cut out ¼in (6mm) beyond the drawn line. Turn the seam allowance to the wrong side of the fabric, tack (baste) it in place and then press (Fig 3). Cut a piece of wadding (batting) the same size as the template and glue it to the top of the steamer basket. Position the stitchery/appliqué on top of the wadding and glue it in place.

Making a twisted cord

9 I made a twisted cord to cover the gap between the stitchery and the basket edge. This looks nice and also covers any imperfections in the basket shape. Use six strands of two different colours of embroidery thread, each about 48in (122cm) long. I used #P10 (antique violet) and #JP12 (seaside). Place the threads together, anchor one end and twist the threads in a clockwise direction until the cord wants to double back on itself. Carefully line up the ends of the threads and let the threads twist. Knot the two ends together. Glue the twisted cord in the groove at the edge of the stitchery and the lip of the lid.

Fig 3

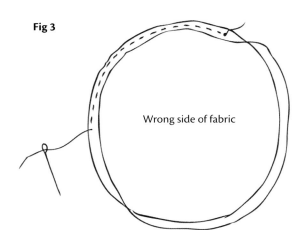

Wrong side of fabric

Lining the inner baskets

10 Steamer baskets are never completely circular, and no two are exactly the same! You will need to determine the size and shape you need to cut the card and wadding (batting) for the base of each basket. Gently press some aluminium foil into the base of basket 1, pressing the foil to the edges and making a crease. Remove the foil and trim it to the shape of the basket base. This is now base template 1, so label this.

11 Using base template 1, cut the following pieces.
❋ Two pieces of thin card (no seam allowance needed).
❋ One piece of wadding (batting) (no seam allowance needed).
❋ Two pieces of cream feature print, adding ½in (1.3cm) seam allowance all round before you cut out the shape.

12 Glue the wadding (batting) to one of the pieces of card. Working on a flat surface, place a piece of the feature print right side down. Centre the wadded card on top, with the wadding facing down. Put a small amount of glue around the outer edge of the card and, working quickly before the glue dries, bring the fabric seam allowance over the edge of the card and press firmly onto the glue. Glue the second piece of fabric in the same way to the other piece of card. Now, with the wrong sides of the covered cards facing each other, glue the two pieces together.

13 To cover the sides of the steamer baskets, measure your baskets. Mine were about 2in (5cm) deep, with an inside circumference of about 22in (56cm). Cut the following pieces (using the measurements of your baskets if different from mine):
❋ One piece of thin card 2in x 22in (5cm x 56cm).
❋ One piece of wadding 2in x 22in (5cm x 56cm).
❋ One piece of purple floral fabric 3in x 24in (7.6cm x 61cm) (includes seam allowance).

14 Glue the wadding (batting) to one side of the card. Working on a flat surface, place the purple floral piece right side down and centre the card with the wadding face down on top of the fabric. Put a small amount of glue on the outer edge of the card, bring the fabric seam allowance over the edge of the card and press firmly onto the glue. Put the completed side lining in place in the basket and then push the covered base lining into position, which will secure it.

15 Repeat Steps 10–14 to line the second steamer basket to finish your sewing basket.

Bird Scissor Holder

You will need...

* Cream-on-cream print for stitchery background 6in (15.2cm) square
* Blue floral fabric 7in (17.8cm) square
* Fusible stitchery stabilizer 6in (15.2cm) square (optional)
* Valdani stranded embroidery threads: #P10 antique violet, #JP12 seaside, #78 aged wine, #P5 tarnished gold, #0511 black sea, #0575 crispy leaf (see Materials & Equipment: Threads for DMC alternatives)
* Thin card (e.g., cereal packet weight)
* Cotton wadding (batting)
* Fine-tipped fabric marking pen (removable if you prefer)
* Fast-tack craft glue suitable for fabric
* Template plastic

Finished size
5½in x 3½in (14cm x 9cm) approx.
Use ¼in (6mm) seams unless otherwise stated

Working the appliqué

1 The scissor keeper uses the same bird appliqué design as the Flower Sewing Basket but a slightly different stitchery design – use the template provided. Using the cream-on-cream stitchery background fabric, add the bird appliqué as described in Step 4 of the Flower Sewing Basket.

Working the stitchery

2 Centre the cream-on-cream background fabric right side up over the stitchery pattern and trace the stitchery lines carefully using a fine-tipped fabric pen. If using an iron-on stitchery stabilizer, fuse it to the back of the fabric before starting the embroidery.

3 Use two strands of embroidery thread. See Basic Techniques: Embroidery Stitches for how to work the stitches, and Materials & Techniques: Threads for DMC alternatives. Stitches used are: backstitch (BS), satin stitch (SS), running stitch (RS), detached lazy daisy (DLD), blanket stitch (BLKS) and French knots (FK). When all embroidery is complete, press carefully.

Making the cord and tassel

4 To make the twisted cord, use six strands of Valdani thread #P10 (antique violet) and #JP12 (seaside), each about 48in (122cm) long. Place the threads together, anchor one end and twist the threads clockwise until the cord wants to double back on itself. Line up the ends of the threads and let the threads twist. Knot the two ends together.

 #P10 Antique violet
Lavender flowers (double row of DLD with FKs along centre)

 #JP12 Seaside
Outer edge of circular flower (BLKS)
Dashed line around flower (RS)
Markings on bird's tail (RS)

 #078 Aged wine
Petals on inner flower (BS)

 #P5 Tarnished gold
Bird's beak (SS)

 #0511 Black sea
Flower centre (BS with four FKs)
Bird eye (FK)
Bird legs (BS)

 #0575 Crispy leaf
Flower stems and leaf (BS)

5 To make the tassel, cut a piece of card 2in (5cm) wide to wrap the threads around. Cut six-stranded lengths of Valdani thread #P10 and #JP12 each at least 60in (152.5cm) long (or longer if you want a fatter tassel). Put them together and wrap them around the card about twelve times (or more), counting wraps from the bottom of the card. When you have reached the desired size, carefully slide the threads off the card and then cut through the bottom loops of the tassel. Take a short length of thread and wrap it around the tassel about ¼in–½in (6mm–1.3cm) down from the top loop. Secure with a knot and thread the ends out of sight. Feed the cord through the loop of the tassel (Fig 1).

Fig 1

Making up the scissor holder

6 Copy the two scissor holder templates onto template plastic. Use these plastic templates to cut the following.

❁ Two back pieces and two front pieces from thin card.

❁ One back piece and one front piece from cotton wadding (batting).

❁ Two back pieces and one front piece from blue floral fabric for lining.

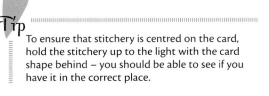
Tip To ensure that stitchery is centred on the card, hold the stitchery up to the light with the card shape behind – you should be able to see if you have it in the correct place.

7 Centre the front template onto the wrong side of your completed stitchery and draw around the template with a pencil. A seam allowance is *not* included on the template, so cut out the shape about ½in (1.3cm) beyond the drawn line all round.

8 Take one back and one front piece of the thin card shape and glue the appropriate wadding (batting) shape to each of them. Place the wadded card shapes onto the wrong sides of the fabric shapes (wadding side to fabric wrong side). Carefully put glue around the edge of the card and then bring the ½in (1.3cm) seam allowance over the edge onto the glue.

9 Once the glue has dried, take both front pieces of the scissor holder and, with wrong sides together, glue the two corresponding pieces together. Hold together whilst the glue is drying. Repeat this process for the back piece but this time sandwich the end of the twisted cord in the centre top, between the two back pieces.

10 Join the front and the back together using two strands of Valdani #P10 antique violet and herringbone stitch (Fig 2). Stitch across the seam of the top front edge first and then all around the edge (see Basic Techniques: Embroidery Stitches). Your scissor holder is now finished.

Fig 2

Little Houses

A red brick house in the country is the dream of many people. If the house can't be a reality then you can make this striking red and cream throw-size quilt instead. It would make a perfect house-warming gift. Two different blocks are used in the quilt, Eight-Point Star and Windmill, and both are straightforward to piece. A further dimension is added to the quilt with the little appliquéd houses in the centre of the star blocks, embellished with sweet touches of embroidery. It would be very easy to change the colour scheme of this quilt, for example using blues instead of reds.

A smaller project features just one appliqué house in a delightful wall hanging. The size is ideal for creating a fast result if you need a gift in a hurry, and the wire hanger is perfect for a country look.

Red House Throw

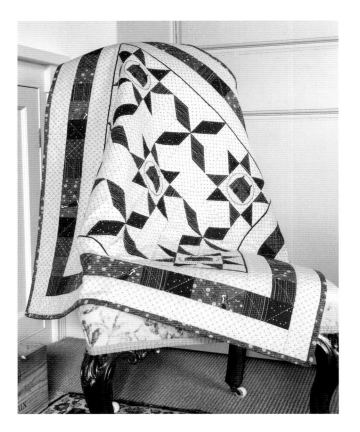

You will need...

❀ Fabric A (I used a red striped print) ¼yd (0.25m)

❀ Fabric B (I used a red star print) ⅜yd (0.4m)

❀ Fabric C (I used a cream print with a fine red grid pattern) 1⅛yd (1.1m)

❀ Three assorted red prints (to use with Fabric A and B for Border 2) ⅛yd (0.125m) of each

❀ Three assorted red fabrics for the house appliqué – you should have sufficient fabric left over from piecing the blocks

❀ Neutral yarn-dyed fine check fabric for appliquéd circles, fat quarter

❀ Fusible stitchery stabilizer (optional)

❀ Stranded embroidery cotton (floss): I used a hand-dyed variegated thread by Cottage Garden Threads #1007 red (or DMC variegated #75) and Cosmo #895 charcoal (or DMC #844)

❀ Template plastic

❀ Fine-tipped fabric marking pen

❀ Light box (optional)

❀ Wadding (batting) 40in (101.5cm) square

❀ Backing fabric 40in (101.5cm) square

❀ Binding fabric (I used a red spot) ⅜yd (0.4m)

Finished size
36½in (92.7cm) square approx.
Use ¼in (6mm) seams unless otherwise stated

Cutting out

1 From Fabric A (red stripe) cut three strips each 3in (7.6cm) x width of fabric. Sub-cut the strips, as follows (keep off-cuts for the appliqué houses):

❀ Eight 3in (7.6cm) squares, for half-square triangle units.

❀ Twenty 2½in (6.4cm) squares for flying geese units.

❀ Twelve 2½in (6.4cm) squares for pieced Border 2.

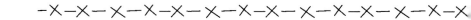

2 From Fabric B (red star) cut four strips each 3in (7.6cm) x width of fabric. Sub-cut three of the strips, as follows. (Keep off-cuts for the houses.)
❀ Eight 3in (7.6cm) squares, for half-square triangle units.
❀ Twenty 2½in (6.4cm) squares for flying geese units.
❀ Twelve 2½in (6.4cm) squares for pieced Border 2. Sub-cut the fourth strip into four lengths each ¾in x 24½in (2cm x 62.2cm) for the folded accent trim.

3 From each of the three assorted red prints, cut one strip 2½in (6.4cm) x width of fabric. Sub-cut each strip into twelve 2½in (6.4cm) squares for pieced Border 2. (Keep off-cuts for the houses.)

4 From Fabric C (cream) cut the following.
❀ Four strips each 2½in (6.4cm) x width of fabric. Sub-cut the strips into twenty rectangles 2½in x 4½in (6.4cm x 11.4cm) for the Eight-Point Star blocks and sixteen rectangles 2½in x 4½in (6.4cm x 11.4cm) for the Windmill blocks.
❀ Cut one strip 3in (7.6cm) x width of fabric and sub-cut into fourteen 3in (7.6cm) squares for half-square triangle units for the Windmill blocks.
❀ Cut one strip 4½in (11.4cm) x width of fabric and sub-cut into five 4½in (11.4cm) squares for the centres of the Eight-Point Star blocks. From the remainder of the strip cut two 3in (7.6cm) squares for half-square triangle units (so you have a total of sixteen 3in/7.6cm squares).

5 From Fabric C (cream) cut eight strips 2½in (6.4cm) x width of fabric and sub-cut as follows.
❀ Two strips 2½in x 24½in (6.4cm x 62.2cm) for Border 1 (top and bottom).
❀ Two strips 2½in x 28½in (6.4cm x 72.4cm) for Border 1 (sides).
❀ Two strips 2½in x 32½in (6.4cm x 82.5cm) for Border 3 (top and bottom).
❀ Two strips 2½in x 36½in (6.4cm x 92.7cm) for Border 3 (sides).
From the remaining Fabric C cut twenty 2½in (6.4cm) squares for the Eight-Point Star blocks.

6 From the binding fabric cut four strips each 2½in (6.4cm) x width of fabric.

Making the Eight-Point Star blocks

7 Start by making the flying geese units (see Basic Techniques: Making a Flying Geese Unit for diagrams if needed). Draw a diagonal line on the wrong side of one Fabric A 2½in (6.4cm) square and one Fabric B square. Pin the Fabric A square, right sides together, with a Fabric C 2½in x 4½in (6.4cm x 11.4cm) rectangle, aligning the left-hand sides, with the drawn line running diagonally from top centre to bottom left corner. Sew on the drawn line. Trim ¼in (6mm) away from the sewn line to remove excess fabric and then press open to reveal the corner triangle.

8 Repeat with the Fabric B square on the other side of the rectangle, but this time sewing along the diagonal from top centre to bottom right corner. Check the flying geese unit is 2½in x 4½in (6.4cm x 11.4cm). Make twenty units like this in total.

9 To assemble a block, take four flying geese units, four 2½in (6.4cm) Fabric C squares and one Fabric C 4½in (11.4cm) square and lay them out as shown in Fig 1A. Sew the units together into rows (1B), pressing the seams towards the darker fabrics. Now sew the rows together (1C). Check the block is 8½in (21.6cm) square. Make four more blocks like this (five in total).

Fig 1
A   B   C

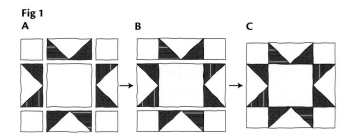

Working the appliqué and stitchery

10 Once the Eight-Point Star blocks have been made you can add the appliqué and embroidery, as follows. From the template plastic create a circle template 3½in (8.9cm) in diameter. Using a suitable fabric marking pen, draw around the circle template on the wrong side of the neutral yarn-dyed check fabric and then cut out ¼in (6mm) beyond the drawn line. Using a light source, such as a light box or a window, centre a circle right side up over the pattern sheet. Trace the stitchery design (French knots circle and chimneys) using a fine-tipped fabric pen. If you are using an iron-on stitchery stabilizer, iron this to the back of the fabric now.

11 Using your favourite method of appliqué, prepare the house pieces. Depending on which type of appliqué you decide to do, you will need to either add a ¼in (6mm) seam allowance to the shapes for traditional needle-turn appliqué or for fusible web appliqué reverse the template shapes before use. I used needle-turn appliqué (see Basic

Techniques: Needle-Turn Appliqué). I used Fabric A for the house roof, Fabric B for the gable and door and another red for the house walls. Using the photos as a guide, position the appliqué shapes. Stitch the shapes in position using a blind hem stitch, using a thread to match the background fabric so it doesn't show.

12 Using a fine-tipped fabric marking pen either freehand draw or trace, with the help of a light box, all the lines for the surface embroidery – window frames, door knob and chimneys. The stitches used are as follows: backstitch (BS), satin stitch (SS) and French knots (FK). Use two strands of stranded cotton (floss). Once stitching is complete, gently press the work.

13 Take the circle with the little house appliqué and turn under about ¼in (6mm) all round the edge and tack (baste) it under. Press carefully. Centre the circle on a star block and appliqué in place using a blind hem stitch. Remove the tacking (basting) stitches. Repeat this process to apply all of the little houses to the quilt.

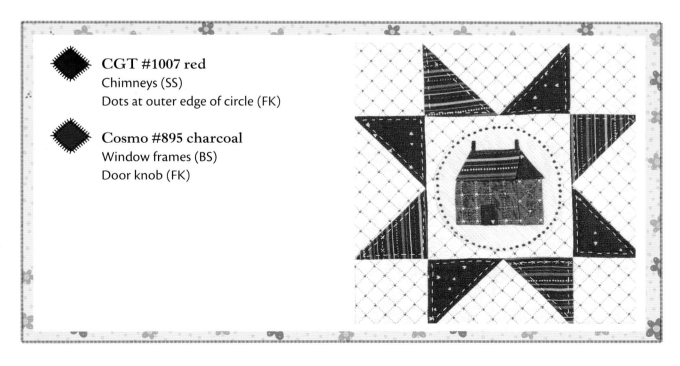

CGT #1007 red
Chimneys (SS)
Dots at outer edge of circle (FK)

Cosmo #895 charcoal
Window frames (BS)
Door knob (FK)

Making the Windmill blocks

14 To make one block, start by making the half-square triangle (HST) units, as follows. Take one Fabric A 3in (7.6cm) square and one Fabric C 3in (7.6cm) square. Draw a diagonal line on the wrong side of the cream square. Pin a red and a cream square, right sides together, and stitch ¼in (6mm) either side of the drawn line (Fig 2A). Cut the unit apart on the line (Fig 2B). Press open and trim each unit to 2½in (6.4cm) square (Fig 2C). Make another two A/B units like this. Repeat the process, this time with Fabric B and Fabric C squares to make four B/C HST units.

Fig 2

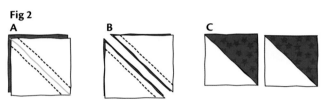

15 Take two A/B HSTs and sew them together as shown in Fig 3A. Sew a 2½in x 4½in (6.4cm x 11.4cm) Fabric C rectangle to the top of the unit. Make another unit like this. Repeat this process with the B/C HSTs (Figs 3A and 3B).

Fig 3

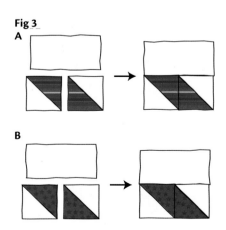

16 Take the four pieced units and arrange them as Fig 4A, making sure that you rotate the units correctly. Sew the units together in pairs and press. Now sew the pairs together and press. Check the block is 8½in (21.6cm) square. Make three more Windmill blocks like this (four in total).

Fig 4

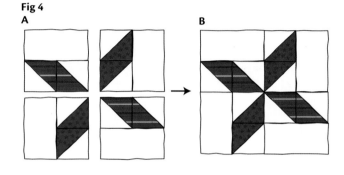

Sewing the blocks together

17 Lay out the blocks into three rows, each with three blocks, alternating the blocks as in Fig 5. Sew the blocks together in rows, pressing the seams of rows 1 and 3 in the opposite direction to row 2. Now sew the rows together, pressing seams in one direction, or open if you prefer. Press the quilt top and check it is 24½in (62.2cm) square.

Fig 5

Adding the trim

18 A narrow splash of red is added around the quilt centre by making a folded trim. Take the four Fabric B ¾in x 24½in (2cm x 62.2cm) strips for the trim, fold the strips in half lengthways, wrong sides together, and press. Align the trim's cut edges to the quilt cut edges on either side of the centre panel. Stitch in place with a ⅛in (3mm) seam. Repeat for the top and bottom of the quilt.

Adding border 1

19 Take the shorter Fabric C strips for Border 1 and sew them to the top and bottom of the quilt. Press seams outwards. Sew the longer strips to the sides of the quilt and press seams outwards.

Adding border 2

20 Border 2 is made up of pieced squares, each 2½in (6.4cm). Take the assorted red print squares you cut earlier and sew them together into two rows, each with fourteen squares, and two rows each with sixteen squares. Press the seams in one direction. Sew the shorter pieced rows to the top and bottom of the quilt and press the seams outwards. Sew the longer pieced rows to the sides of the quilt and press the seams outwards.

Adding border 3

21 Take the shorter Fabric C strips for Border 3 and sew them to the top and bottom of the quilt. Press the seams outwards. Sew the longer strips to the sides of the quilt and press the seams outwards.

Quilting and finishing

22 Lay the pressed backing right side down, with the smoothed wadding (batting) on top. Lay the quilt top right side up on top, making sure there is wadding and backing showing all round, and then secure the quilt layers together (see Basic Techniques: Making a Quilt Sandwich).

23 Quilt as desired. I used an invisible thread to hand quilt around the circles and off-white thread to hand quilt the red fabric shapes, about ⅛in (3mm) away from the seams. The pieced squares border has diagonal hand quilting in a zigzag pattern along the squares.

24 When all quilting is finished, tidy all thread ends, square up the quilt and prepare for binding. Join the binding fabric strips together end to end using 45-degree seams. Press the seams open. Fold the strip in half all along the length, wrong sides together and press. Use this strip to bind your quilt – see Basic Techniques: Binding.

Little House Wall Hanging

You will need...

❈ Background fabric (I used a cream print with a fine red grid pattern) 6in (15.2cm) square

❈ Neutral yarn-dyed fine check fabric 5in (12.7cm) square

❈ Three assorted red prints for house appliqué, about 3in (7.6cm) square of each

❈ Fusible stitchery stabilizer (optional)

❈ Stranded embroidery cotton (floss): I used a hand-dyed variegated thread by Cottage Garden Threads #1007 red (or DMC variegated #75) and Cosmo #895 charcoal (or DMC #844)

❈ Template plastic

❈ Fine-tipped fabric marking pen

❈ Roxanne's Glue Baste It™ (optional)

❈ Light box or light pad (optional)

❈ Wadding (batting) 7in (17.8cm) square

❈ Backing 10in (25.4cm) square (includes an amount for a hanging sleeve)

❈ Binding fabric (I used a red stripe) 2½in x 30in (6.4cm x 76cm)

❈ Wirework hanger (see Suppliers)

Finished size
6in (15.2cm) square approx.
Use ¼in (6mm) seams unless otherwise stated

Working the appliqué and stitchery

1 From template plastic make a 3½in (8.9cm) diameter circle template. Prepare a background circle using the neutral yarn-dyed check fabric. Using a suitable fabric marking pen, draw around the circle template on the wrong side of the fabric and then cut out ¼in (6mm) beyond the drawn line. Using a light source, such as a light box, light pad or a window, centre a circle, right side up, over the pattern sheet. Trace the stitchery design using a fine-tipped fabric pen. If you are using an iron-on stitchery stabilizer, iron this to the back of the fabric now.

—✕—✕—✕—✕—✕—✕—✕—✕—✕—✕—✕—✕—✕—✕—

2 Using your favourite method of appliqué, prepare the house pieces. Depending on the type of appliqué chosen, you will need to either add a ¼in (6mm) seam allowance to the shapes for traditional needle-turn appliqué or, for fusible web appliqué, you will need to reverse the template shapes before use. I used needle-turn appliqué (see Basic Techniques: Needle-Turn Appliqué). I used a striped red fabric for the house roof, a red star print for the gable and door, and another red for the walls. Using the picture as a guide, position the appliqué shapes. Stitch the shapes in position with a blind hem stitch, using a thread to match the background fabric so it doesn't show.

3 Using a fine-tipped fabric marking pen either freehand draw or trace, with the help of a light source, all the lines for the surface embroidery – window frames, door knob and chimneys. The stitches used are as follows: backstitch (BS), satin stitch (SS), and French knots (FK). Use two strands of stranded cotton (floss) unless otherwise stated. Once stitching is complete, gently press the work.

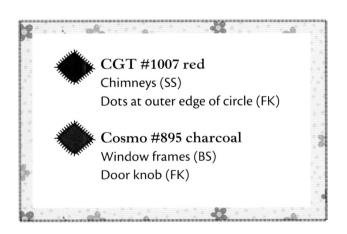

CGT #1007 red
Chimneys (SS)
Dots at outer edge of circle (FK)

Cosmo #895 charcoal
Window frames (BS)
Door knob (FK)

4 Take the circle with the house appliqué and turn under about ¼in (6mm) all round the edge and tack (baste) it under. Press carefully. Centre the circle on the background square and appliqué in place with a blind hem stitch. Remove tacking (basting) stitches.

Quilting and finishing

5 Lay the pressed backing right side down, with the smoothed wadding (batting) on top. Lay the wall hanging right side up on top, making sure there is wadding and backing showing all round, and then secure the layers together (see Basic Techniques: Making a Quilt Sandwich).

6 Quilt as desired. I used an invisible thread to hand quilt around the circle.

7 When the quilting is finished, tidy all thread ends, square up the wall hanging if needed and prepare for binding. Fold the binding strip in half all along the length, wrong sides together, and press. Use this strip to bind your wall hanging – see Basic Techniques: Binding.

8 I made a hanging sleeve for this project so it could be displayed on a wirework hanger. Cut a piece of backing fabric about 2½in x 4½in (6.4cm x 11.4cm). Turn under a ¼in (6mm) hem at each end and sew in place. Fold the fabric in half along the length, wrong sides together, and sew along one long edge. Turn the tube through to the right side and press. Hand sew the sleeve in place below the binding on the back, making sure your stitches don't show on the front.

Winter Star

Warm and cool fabric tones come together to create this lovely shoulder bag. Five of the blocks are created with eight-point stars, which have been hand pieced and then accented with little buttons. The bird and flower appliqué design is created with a traditional needle-turn appliqué technique. A domed circle of embroidery decorates the flap and a robust strap in faux leather makes the bag highly practical.

The sweet little purse, ideal for keys or a few coins, matches the colours of the bag and is the perfect accompaniment. It features a charming appliqué scene of two tiny birds.

Winter Star Handbag

You will need...

❊ Brown/red heart print for star background 6in (15.2cm) x width of fabric

❊ Brown texture print for bag flap, flap lining and star block background 6in (15.2cm) x width of fabric

❊ Cream-on-cream stripe, for bird block background and covered dome 9in (22.9cm) square

❊ Brown floral print for front and back of bag 10in (25.5cm) x width of fabric

❊ Tan floral fabric for bag lining 10in (25.5cm) x width of fabric

❊ Lightweight fusible wadding (batting) about 30in (76cm) square

❊ Valdani stranded embroidery cotton (floss): #578 primitive blue, #078 aged wine, #154 antique gold, #P10 antique violet, #H212 faded brown, #519 olive green (see Materials & Equipment: Threads for DMC alternatives)

❊ Fine-tipped fabric marking pen (removable if you prefer)

❊ Fusible stitchery stabilizer (optional)

❊ Template plastic

❊ Stitch-on magnetic clasp

❊ Two D-rings for handle

❊ Commercial leather-type shoulder strap (see Suppliers)

❊ Five tiny buttons

❊ Plastic dome, to cover embroidery 1½in (3.8cm) diameter (see Suppliers)

Finished size
8in x 8½in (20.3cm x 21.6cm) excluding handles
Use ¼in (6mm) seams unless otherwise stated

Transferring the stitchery design

1 From the cream-on-cream stripe fabric cut one 4in (10.2cm) square for the background of the bird block. Copy the stitchery and appliqué template from the Templates section. Using a light source, such as a light box or a window, centre the striped square right side up over the pattern and use a fine-tipped fabric marking pen to carefully trace the stitchery lines.

Tip

If you are unable to see though your background fabric to trace the design then try drawing over the pattern lines with a thicker felt-tip pen as this will show through the fabric more easily.

−✕−✕− ✕−✕−✕− ✕−✕−✕− ✕−✕−✕−✕−✕−✕−✕

Working the appliqué

2 You can do the appliqué before or after the stitchery has been completed – I prefer to do my appliqué before. Using your favourite method of appliqué, apply the hill and the bird. If using fusible web appliqué, reverse the shapes before using. I made templates for the appliqué shapes from paper, drew around the templates onto the wrong side of my chosen fabrics and cut out the pieces out adding a ¼in (6mm) seam allowance. I then used needle-turn appliqué and blind hem stitch with matching thread to sew the bird in place (see Techniques: Appliqué). Press the sewn shapes, first on the wrong side and then on the right side.

Working the stitchery

3 If using an iron-on stitchery stabilizer, fuse it to the back of the fabric before the embroidery.

4 Using a fine-tipped fabric marking pen transfer the surface stitchery lines for the heart on the bird either freehand or using a light box.

5 Use two strands of Valdani embroidery thread. See Basic Techniques: Embroidery Stitches for how to work the stitches and Materials & Equipment: Threads for DMC alternatives. Stitches used are (abbreviations in brackets): backstitch (BS), satin stitch (SS), running stitch (RS), detached lazy daisy (DLD) and French knots (FK). When all the embroidery is complete, press the work carefully.

Tip
I like to use Roxanne's Glue Baste It ™ to fix the shapes in position on the background. You could use pins but I don't like the way the thread gets caught around the pins.

 #578 Primitive blue
Dots in sky (FK)
Petals on right-hand daisy (SS)

#078 Aged wine
Heart on bird (SS)

 #154 Antique gold
Bird beak (BS)
Fill daisy centres (FK)

#P10 Antique violet
Petals on three left-hand daisies (SS)

 #H212 Faded brown
Bird legs (BS)
Bird eye (FK)
Tail feather markings (RS)

 #519 Olive green
Leaves around daisies (DLD)

Making the Eight-Point Star blocks

6 There are five of these blocks on the bag, each 3½in (8.9cm) square. Two of the star blocks are a red/brown fabric combination and three are a blue/brown combination. Copy the square, diamond and triangle templates provided onto template plastic. Use these plastic templates to cut out the fabric pieces, cutting out with an extra ¼in (6mm) all round for a seam allowance. For each block you will need four squares, four triangles and eight diamonds.

7 Hand piece a star block as in Fig 1. (See also Basic Techniques: English Paper Piecing.) The sewn block will look like Fig 1C. Repeat to make five stars in total. Check each block is 3½in (8.9cm) square. Sew a small button in the centre of each star block.

Fig 1

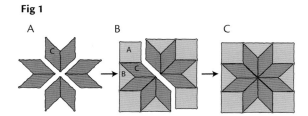

Assembling the bag front

8 Trim the bird block to 3½in (8.9cm) square. Using the picture as a guide, arrange the star blocks and the bird block in two rows. Sew the blocks together with ¼in (6mm) seams, pressing the seams in opposite directions. Now sew the rows together (Fig 2).

Fig 2

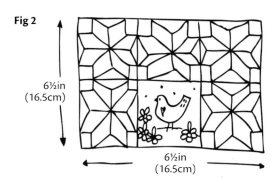

9 From brown floral fabric cut a rectangle 3½in x 9½in (8.9cm x 24.1cm) and sew this to the top of the patchwork (Fig 3). Cut a piece of wadding (batting) slightly larger than this whole front piece.

Fig 3

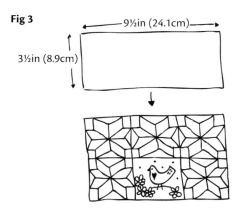

10 Place the whole bag front piece, right side up, on the wadding (batting) and press to fuse in place. Quilt as desired. For example, you could quilt in the seam ditches of the blocks and around the star block shapes. Now cut out the shape of the bag front using the template for the front of the bag.

-X—X—X—X—X—X—X—X—X—X—X—X—X—X—X

Making the back of the bag

11 From brown floral fabric and fusible wadding (batting) cut a 10in (25.5cm) square. Fuse the wadding to the wrong side of the fabric. Quilt a simple cross-hatch pattern.

12 Cut out the shape of the bag back using the template for the back of the bag. Stitch the two darts where shown on the template. Place the back and the front of the bag right sides together, aligning the top edges and curved sides, and stitch together with a ¼in (6mm) seam all around the curved edge (Fig 4). The stitched darts will give a fuller appearance to the back of the bag. Turn through to the right side and press the seam.

13 From the tan floral fabric cut two lining pieces using the templates, as before. Stitch the darts, as before. Place the two lining pieces right sides together, aligning the top and curved edges, and sew together, leaving an opening for turning the bag through to the right side (Fig 5). Press the seam and

place the lining inside the bag, with outer right sides together (Fig 6). Line up the top edges and side seams and stitch around the top of the bag ¼in (6mm) from the edge (Fig 7). Turn to the right side through the lining opening. Stitch the opening closed.

Making the covered dome

14 Cut a 3in (7.6cm) square from the cream stripe fabric and transfer the stitchery design to the right side of the fabric. If using a fusible stitchery stabilizer, bond this to wrong side of fabric before starting the embroidery. Work the flower embroidery as for the bird block, using two strands of thread. Use faded brown for the running stitch circle.

15 Once the stitching has been completed, use the flap circle stitchery template to cut out the shape. Work a row of gathering stitches around the circle and draw it up so it fits tightly around the plastic dome (Fig 8). Fasten the thread securely.

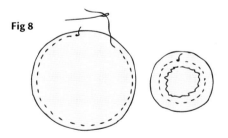

Fig 8

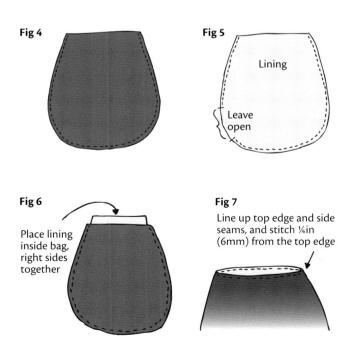

Fig 4

Fig 5
Lining
Leave open

Fig 6
Place lining inside bag, right sides together

Fig 7
Line up top edge and side seams, and stitch ¼in (6mm) from the top edge

Making and attaching the bag flap

16 Copy the template for the bag flap and cut two from the brown texture print and one from wadding (batting). Place the fabric right sides together with the wadding on the top and machine stitch around the curve. Clip into the curve (Fig 9). Turn through to the right side and press. With two strands of #078 aged wine stranded cotton (floss), work a large running stitch about ¼in (6mm) in from the edge through all layers. Stitch the covered dome into position on the flap (Fig 10).

Fig 9

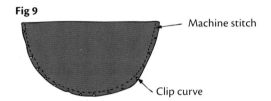

Machine stitch

Clip curve

Fig 10

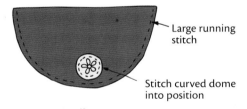

Large running stitch

Stitch curved dome into position

17 From the tan floral fabric cut two pieces each 1¼in x 7in (3.2cm x 17.8cm). Place the pieces right sides together and stitch around the entire shape. Cut a slit through one layer only (Fig 11A). Turn through to right side and press (Fig 11B).

Fig 11

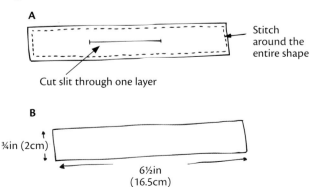

A

Cut slit through one layer

Stitch around the entire shape

B

¾in (2cm)

6½in (16.5cm)

18 Make four loops to hold the D-rings by cutting a strip from tan floral 1½in x 6in (3.8cm x 15.2cm). Fold the fabric in half lengthwise, right sides together, and stitch together along the length (Fig 12). Turn through to the right side and press. Cut into four equal pieces, fold each piece in half and press to make four loops.

Fig 12

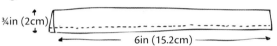

¾in (2cm)

6in (15.2cm)

19 Position the loops on the wrong side of the flap attachment. Slide the D-rings in place, pin and use matching thread to neatly stitch the loops in place so they cannot move (Fig 13).

Fig 13

Machine stitch to hold loops in place

20 Take the bag and the bag flap. Open the bag and place the bag flap about ½in (1.3cm) down on the inside back of the bag. Pin in position. Now cover the raw edge of the bag flap with the flap attachment piece and machine stitch the layers together (Fig 14). Stitch the magnetic clasp in place. Clip the ready-made bag handles onto the D-rings and enjoy your bag.

Fig 14

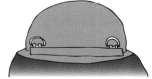

—✕—✕—✕—✕—✕—✕—✕—✕—✕—✕—✕—✕—✕—✕—

Two Little Birds Purse

You will need...

❀ Cream stripe print for stitchery background 6in (15.2cm) square

❀ Brown floral print for back of purse 6in (15.2cm) square

❀ Blue floral fabric for bird appliqué 1½in x 3½in (3.8cm x 8.9cm)

❀ Grey print for hill 1½in x 5in (3.8cm x 12.7cm)

❀ Tan floral lining fabric 8in x 6in (20.3cm x 15.2cm)

❀ Blue print for bias binding 11in (28cm) square

❀ Fusible stabilizer (optional) 6in (15.2cm) square

❀ Lightweight fusible wadding (batting) (I used Pellon) 8in x 6in (20.3cm x 15.2cm)

❀ Valdani stranded embroidery cotton (floss): #578 primitive blue, #078 aged wine, #154 antique gold, #P10 antique violet, H212 faded brown (see Materials & Equipment: Threads for DMC alternatives)

❀ Fine-tipped fabric marking pen (removable if you prefer)

❀ Template plastic

❀ Masking tape ½in (1.3cm) wide as a quilting guide (optional)

❀ Antique gold-coloured zip 5in (12.7cm) long

Finished size
4¼in x 2½in (11cm x 6.5cm) approx.
Use ¼in (6mm) seams unless otherwise stated

Making bias binding

1 Take the 11in (28cm) square of blue print and cut it into 1¼in (3.2cm) wide bias strips, as described in Basic Techniques: Cutting Bias Strips. Join the strips with ¼in (6mm) seams to make a length of at least 20in (51cm). Fold and press over about ¼in (6mm) of the fabric along the entire length, wrong sides together. Put aside for later.

Making the purse

2 From template plastic make templates for both sections of the purse (A and B) using the patterns provided. Trace around template A onto the cream stitchery background fabric and cut out on the line (the seam allowances have been included in the templates). Trace around template B on the brown floral fabric and cut out on the line. Join fabric A piece and fabric B piece together (Fig 1).

Fig 1

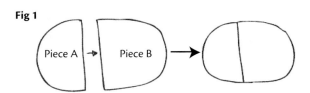

Transferring the stitchery design

3 Using a light source, such as a light box or window, centre the cream background fabric right side up over the stitchery pattern. Use a fine-tipped fabric marker to carefully trace the stitchery lines. If using an iron-on stitchery stabilizer, fuse it into place before starting the embroidery.

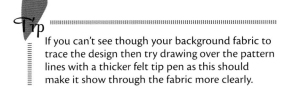

Tip
If you can't see though your background fabric to trace the design then try drawing over the pattern lines with a thicker felt tip pen as this should make it show through the fabric more clearly.

Working the appliqué

4 You can do the appliqué either before or after the stitchery has been completed. I prefer to do my appliqué before. Using your favourite method of appliqué, apply the hill and the birds. See Step 2 of the Winter Star Handbag for the method I used. When the appliqué is complete, use a fine-tipped fabric marker to transfer the surface stitchery lines for the hearts and tail markings, either freehand or using a light box.

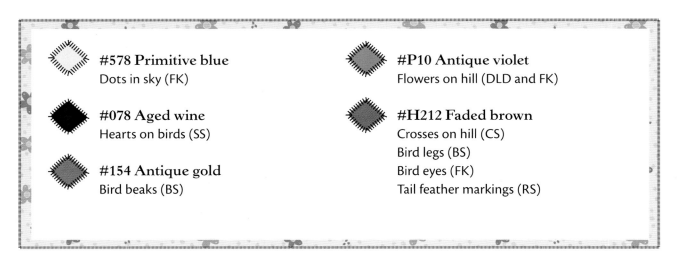

#578 **Primitive blue**
Dots in sky (FK)

#078 **Aged wine**
Hearts on birds (SS)

#154 **Antique gold**
Bird beaks (BS)

#P10 **Antique violet**
Flowers on hill (DLD and FK)

#H212 **Faded brown**
Crosses on hill (CS)
Bird legs (BS)
Bird eyes (FK)
Tail feather markings (RS)

Working the stitchery

5 Use two strands of Valdani embroidery thread. See Basic Techniques: Embroidery Stitches for how to work the stitches and Materials & Equipment: Threads for DMC alternatives. Stitches used are (abbreviations in brackets): backstitch (BS), satin stitch (SS), cross stitch (CS), running stitch (RS), detached lazy daisy (DLD) and French knots (FK). When all embroidery is complete press the work carefully.

Making up the purse

6 Take the fusible wadding (batting) and lining fabric and bond the wadding to the wrong side of the lining. Place the stitched purse outer piece right side up on the wadding. Machine quilt a cross-hatch pattern, using ½in (1.3cm) wide masking tape, or other marking method of your choice. Once the quilting is finished trim the wadding and lining to the same size as the stitched purse outer (Fig 2).

Fig 2

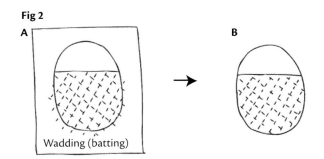

A

B

Wadding (batting)

7 Take some of the bias binding prepared earlier and bind the edge of the oval (Fig 3), placing the binding right sides together with the purse, and matching the top curve of the purse.

Fig 3

8 Check the length of the zip and mark with a pin where it will start and stop. Hand stitch the side of the purse together, and repeat for other side (Fig 4). Place the zip in position and backstitch it into place, first on one side and then the other (Fig 5). To make the inside of the purse neat, stitch the selvedge side of the zip carefully to the purse lining.

Fig 4

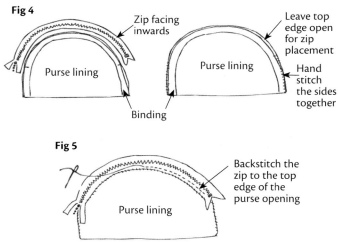

Zip facing inwards

Leave top edge open for zip placement

Purse lining

Purse lining

Hand stitch the sides together

Binding

Fig 5

Backstitch the zip to the top edge of the purse opening

Purse lining

9 To make a base to the purse, fold and machine stitch across the corner on both sides (Fig 6). Turn your purse to the right side and enjoy!

Fig 6

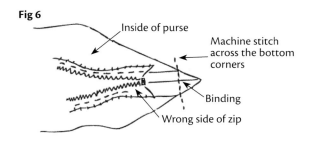

Inside of purse

Machine stitch across the bottom corners

Binding

Wrong side of zip

Country Friends

Sweet stitcheries combined with paper-pieced triangles and hexagons will make this lovely table topper a focal point in your dining room – perfect for when entertaining friends. It is created using traditional English paper piecing, with hexagons made up of triangles in alternating colours. The delightful teacup full of flowers is worked in simple embroidery stitches, making this project suitable for all levels of ability. Why not make it in different colours to suit each season?

Individual hexagon-shaped coasters make an ideal match for the table topper and are sure to delight your guests. I made an assortment of six coasters – plain ones that show off a gorgeous print, triangle-pieced hexagon ones and a sweet stitchery version. You can mix and match as I have done, or make a matching set.

Friends Table Topper

You will need...

❀ Cream-on-cream fabric for stitchery background, fat quarter

❀ Blue focus print for large hexagons, fat eighth

❀ Blue checked print for centre hexagon, border triangles and binding, ¼yd (0.25m)

❀ Four different prints for triangle hexagons (two darks and two lights), fat eighth of each

❀ Burgundy print for backing fabric 20in (51cm) square

❀ Wadding (batting) 20in (51cm) square

❀ Seventy-two pre-cut paper equilateral triangles with 2in (5cm) sides (or use template supplied)

❀ Thirteen pre-cut paper hexagons with 2in (5cm) sides (or use template supplied) – six of these will be cut up to create border triangles

❀ Fusible stitchery stabilizer, 15in (38cm) square (optional)

❀ Valdani stranded embroidery cotton (floss): #31 tealish blue, #78 aged wine, #512 chimney dust, #514 wheat husk, #539 evergreens, #548 blackened khaki and #8103 withered mulberry (see Materials & Equipment: Threads for DMC alternatives)

❀ Fine-tipped fabric marker

❀ Basting glue (optional)

❀ Fabric glue pen (optional)

❀ Light box or light pad (optional)

Finished size
17½in x 16½in (44.5cm x 42cm) approx.
Use ¼in (6mm) seams unless otherwise stated

Transferring the stitchery design

1 Copy the flowers in a teacup stitchery pattern from the Templates section. Using a light source, such as a light box/pad or window, place the cream-on-cream stitchery background fabric right side up over the pattern, allowing enough room to trace the design three times in total. Leave enough space between the designs (including a seam allowance all round) so you can cut them apart later. Trace the stitchery lines carefully using a fine-tipped fabric pen.

-X-X- X-X-X- X-X-X- X-X-X- X-X-X

Working the stitchery

2 If you are using a fusible stitchery stabilizer, fuse it to the back of the fabric before starting the embroidery. Using this will also avoid thread shadows showing on the front of your work. Place the shiny side of the stabilizer on to the wrong side of your fabric and bond it in place with an iron, following the manufacturer's instructions.

3 Use two strands of Valdani embroidery thread. See Basic Techniques: Embroidery Stitches for how to work the stitches and Materials & Equipment: Threads for DMC alternatives. Stitches used are (abbreviations in brackets): backstitch (BS), satin stitch (SS), cross stitch (CS), detached lazy daisy (DLD), running stitch (RS) and French knots (FK). When all embroidery is complete press the work carefully.

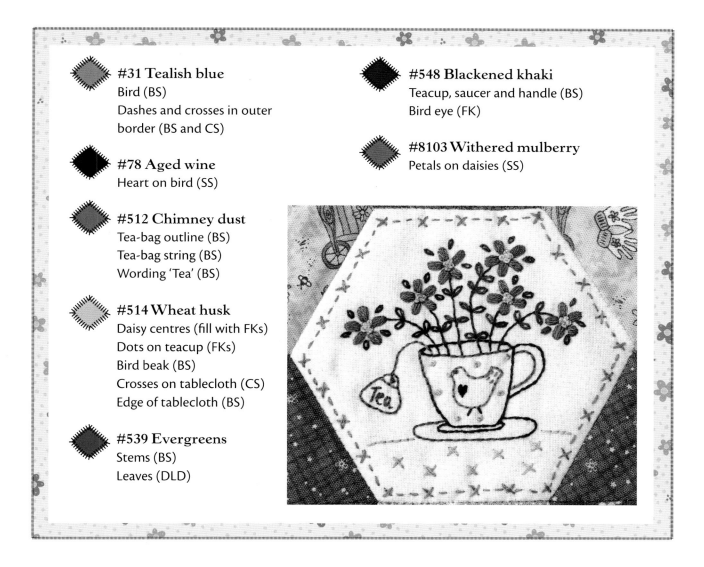

#31 Tealish blue
Bird (BS)
Dashes and crosses in outer border (BS and CS)

#78 Aged wine
Heart on bird (SS)

#512 Chimney dust
Tea-bag outline (BS)
Tea-bag string (BS)
Wording 'Tea' (BS)

#514 Wheat husk
Daisy centres (fill with FKs)
Dots on teacup (FKs)
Bird beak (BS)
Crosses on tablecloth (CS)
Edge of tablecloth (BS)

#539 Evergreens
Stems (BS)
Leaves (DLD)

#548 Blackened khaki
Teacup, saucer and handle (BS)
Bird eye (FK)

#8103 Withered mulberry
Petals on daisies (SS)

Paper piecing the triangles

4 Using the pre-cut paper equilateral triangles (or creating your own using the template supplied), prepare eighteen fabric triangles from each of the four different prints, using an English paper piecing technique (see Basic Techniques: English Paper Piecing for details). Each triangle will need a starting square of fabric about 2½in (6.4cm) square, which allows enough extra for a seam allowance all round. Fig 1 shows the basic stages for creating the fabric triangles.

Fig 1

A

B

C

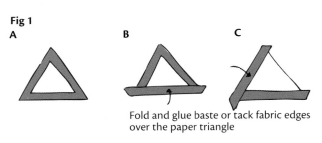

Fold and glue baste or tack fabric edges over the paper triangle

D

E

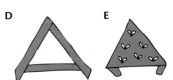

5 Using small slipstitches and matching thread, join six fabric triangles together to form one hexagon with 2in (5cm) sides. I alternated two prints within one hexagon (see Fig 2 and photos). Make twelve hexagons in total – six with dark prints and six with light prints. Press the shapes well and then remove the paper templates.

Fig 2

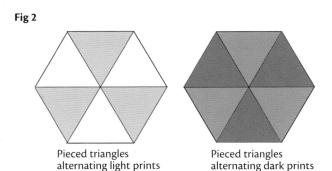

Pieced triangles alternating light prints

Pieced triangles alternating dark prints

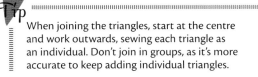

Tip When joining the triangles, start at the centre and work outwards, sewing each triangle as an individual. Don't join in groups, as it's more accurate to keep adding individual triangles.

—✕—✕—✕—✕—✕—✕—✕—✕—✕—✕—✕—✕—✕—✕—

Preparing the other hexagons

6 Prepare the following hexagons using the same English paper piecing technique. When these are prepared you will have nineteen hexagons in total.

❋ Three hexagons with 2in (5cm) sides in blue focus print.

❋ Three hexagons using the stitcheries.

❋ One central hexagon in blue check print.

On the central hexagon add some embroidery around the edge using #31 tealish blue stranded cotton (floss) and stitching the same dashed line and cross stitch pattern as the stitchery hexagons.

Making the border triangles

7 The border triangle template can be made in one of two ways: copying the template provided, or cutting up pre-cut hexagons into triangle shapes. If using pre-cut shapes, cut up six of the 2in (5cm) paper hexagons to make the triangles as in Fig 3. Discard the central piece of paper. Once the border triangle templates are prepared, cover them with the blue check fabric using English paper piecing as before.

Making up the topper

8 Take all of the prepared hexagons and the outer triangles and lay them out as shown in the photograph. Sew the pieces together using small slipstitches and matching thread. Press the work.

9 Place the backing fabric square right side down, add the wadding (batting) on top and then the patchwork right side up. Tack (baste) or pin the layers together and then quilt as desired. I machine quilted in the ditch around the central hexagon and also around the second round of hexagons, using an invisible thread. Tidy all thread ends and then trim the backing and wadding to the same shape as the topper.

10 To bind the table topper cut two strips from the blue check fabric, on the straight grain, each 2in (5cm) x width of fabric. Join the strips together and press the seams open. You will need about 60in (152cm) in total. Fold the strip in half along the length, right sides together, and press. Bind your table topper to finish (see Basic Techniques: Binding).

Fig 3 Creating the outer triangle template by cutting down a pre-cut hexagon

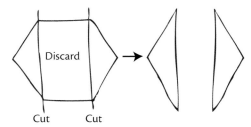

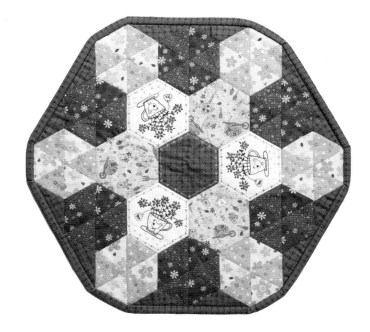

Teatime Coasters

You will need...

For each coaster
❋ Blue check print for coaster base and backing 6½in (16.5cm)
❋ Light wadding (batting) 6½in (16.5cm) square
❋ Template plastic (optional)

For one plain hexagon coaster
❋ Blue focus print 5in (12.7cm) square
❋ One pre-cut paper hexagon with 2in (5cm) sides (or use Friends Table Topper template)

For one stitchery coaster
❋ Cream-on-cream fabric for stitchery background 5in (12.7cm) square
❋ Fusible stitchery stabilizer 5in (12.7cm) square (optional)
❋ Valdani stranded embroidery cotton (floss): #31 tealish blue, #78 aged wine, #512 chimney dust, #514 wheat husk, #539 evergreens, #548 blackened khaki and #8103 withered mulberry (see the Materials & Equipment: Threads for DMC alternatives)
❋ One pre-cut paper hexagon with 2in (5cm) sides (or use Friends Table Topper template)

For one pieced hexagon coaster
❋ Two coordinating prints, one 6in (15.2cm) square of each
❋ Six pre-cut paper equilateral triangles with 2in (5cm) sides (or use Friends Table Topper template)

Finished size for each coaster
4½in x 5in (11.4cm x 12.7cm) approx.
Use ¼in (6mm) seams unless otherwise stated

Making a coaster base

1 All three versions of the coaster are made with the same base shape, with smaller hexagons appliquéd on top, which then gives the appearance of a border around the coaster. Using the coaster base template supplied, cut two shapes from the blue check print and one from wadding (batting). The template includes a generous ¼in (6mm) seam allowance.

2 Place one blue check hexagon right side up and then the other hexagon on top, right side down. Add the wadding hexagon on top of this, aligning all edges neatly. Pin together and then machine stitch around the entire shape. Cut a small slit through just one layer of the blue check fabric (Fig 1). Turn the hexagon to the right side, through the slit and press. This slit will be covered by a smaller hexagon later.

−✕−✕− ✕−✕−✕− ✕−✕−✕− ✕−✕−✕− ✕−✕−

Fig 1

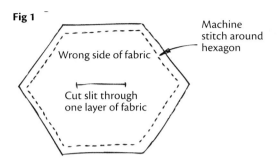

Machine stitch around hexagon

Wrong side of fabric

Cut slit through one layer of fabric

Making the plain coaster

3 Make a base coaster as in Steps 1 and 2. Use the pre-cut 2in (5cm) hexagon to paper piece the blue focus fabric. Alternatively, use the paper and fabric hexagon templates supplied in the Templates section. Press the prepared fabric hexagon and then sew it to the centre of the base hexagon (covering the slit), using matching thread and small slipstitches.

Making the stitchery coaster

4 Make a base coaster as in Steps 1 and 2. Following Steps 1–3 of the Friends Table Topper project, work the stitchery on the cream-on-cream fabric square, marking and stitching the design just once. Use the pre-cut 2in hexagon to paper piece the stitchery (or use the templates in the Templates section). Sew the stitchery hexagon to the centre of the base hexagon (covering the slit), using matching thread and small slipstitches.

Making the pieced hexagon coaster

5 Make a base coaster as in Steps 1 and 2. Following Steps 4 and 5 of the Friends Table Topper project, create a pieced hexagon from the triangles. Press well and then remove the papers. Sew the pieced hexagon to the centre of the base hexagon (covering the slit), using matching thread and small slipstitches.

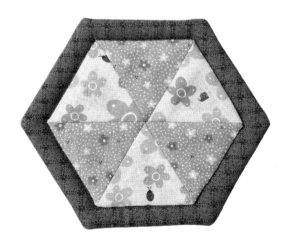

Quilting and finishing

6 For all coasters, press the coasters and then use machine quilting and invisible thread to quilt around the edge of each inner hexagon. Tidy all threads ends by burying them inside the coasters.

Alphabet Sampler

This pretty pillow evokes memories of cross stitch alphabet samplers worked in centuries past. The embroidery stitches are simple ones, but coupled with the pot of flowers, a hand-painted daisy button and the appliquéd birds, the overall effect is utterly charming. Two rows of small half-square triangles bring additional interest and colour to the design. If giving this pillow as a gift it would be easy to change the fabrics to suit the colour preferences of the recipient.

A small but exquisite mini cushion accompanies the pillow using the same bird appliqué. It would make a lovely gift and you could use it as a pincushion or put some fragrant pot-pourri in the stuffing so it becomes a scented sachet. The heart-shaped embroidery design would look so pretty on other projects, too.

Alphabet Sampler Pillow

You will need...

❀ Cream yarn-dyed fabric for background 5in x 10in (12.7cm x 24.5cm) – the one I used has a light grid pattern on it

❀ Brown floral fabric 1in (2.5cm) x width of fabric

❀ Blue stripe fabric 2in x 19in (5cm x 48.3cm)

❀ Blue print for bird appliqué 2in x 4in (5cm x 10.2cm)

❀ Mauve print for bird wings 1in x 3in (2.5cm x 7.6cm)

❀ Burgundy swirl print for trim ¾in x 20in (2cm x 50.8cm) and three 5in (12.7cm) squares for half-square triangles

❀ Burgundy stripe fabric for pot 2in (5cm) square

❀ Green print for half-square triangles three 5in (12.7cm) squares

❀ Blue swirl print for pillow sides and backing 9½in (24.1cm) x width of fabric

❀ Valdani stranded embroidery cotton (floss): #P10 antique violet, #031 tealish blue, #0503 garnets, #0575 crispy leaf, #0511 black sea, #0154 antique gold and #0518 dusty leaves (see Materials & Equipment: Threads for DMC alternatives)

❀ Fusible stitchery stabilizer (optional) 5in x 10in (12.7cm x 24.5cm)

❀ Fusible lightweight wadding (batting) two pieces 10in x 17in (25.5cm x 43.2cm)

❀ Roxanne's Glue Baste It ™ (optional)

❀ One daisy button (see Suppliers)

❀ Fine-tipped fabric marking pen

❀ Toy filling for stuffing

Finished size
16in x 9in (40.6cm x 22.9cm) approx.
Use ¼in (6mm) seams unless otherwise stated

Transferring the design

1 Copy the pattern from the Templates section. Using a light source, such as a light box/pad or window, place the cream background fabric centrally, right side up, over the pattern. Carefully trace the stitchery lines onto the fabric using a fine-tipped fabric pen.

—X—X—X—X—X—X—X—X—X—X—X—X—X—

2 If you are using a fusible stitchery stabilizer, fuse it to the back of the fabric before starting the embroidery. Using this will also avoid thread shadows showing on the front of your work. Place the shiny side of the stabilizer on to the wrong side of your fabric and bond it in place with an iron, following the manufacturer's instructions. You can do the appliqué now or after the stitchery has been completed – I prefer to do my appliqué before the stitchery.

Working the appliqué

3 Using your favourite method of appliqué, prepare the birds, wings and pot using the templates supplied. Depending on which type of appliqué you decide to do, you will need to either add a ¼in (6mm) seam allowance to the shapes for needle-turn appliqué or, for fusible web appliqué, reverse the template shapes before use. I used needle-turn appliqué (see Basic Techniques: Needle-Turn Appliqué).

4 Using the pictures as a guide, position the birds onto your background fabric. With this simple design it should be easy to place the motifs. Once you are happy with their positions, glue baste or pin the appliqué shapes in place. Stitch them with a blind hem stitch, using a thread to match the background fabric so it doesn't show.

Tip

When using traditional needle-turn appliqué, I use a basting glue to fix the shapes in position on the background. Roxanne's Glue Baste It ™ has a small tube through which tiny drops of glue emerge, allowing for fine placement of the glue. You could use pins but I don't like the way the thread gets caught around the pins as I'm sewing.

5 Using a fine-tipped fabric marking pen, either freehand draw or trace the lines for the surface embroidery (two hearts) onto the appliqués.

Working the stitchery

6 Use two strands of Valdani embroidery thread. See Basic Techniques: Embroidery Stitches for how to work the stitches and the Materials & Equipment: Threads for DMC alternatives. Stitches used are: backstitch (BS), satin stitch (SS), running stitch (RS), cross stitch (CS), detached lazy daisy (DLD) and French knots (FK). When all embroidery is complete press the work carefully. Trim the panel to 4½in x 9½in (11.4cm x 24.1cm).

#P10 Antique violet
Berries on stems (FK)
Cross stitches above alphabet (CS)

#031 Tealish blue
Daisy outlines (BS)
Dots on daisies (FK)
Heart on pot (SS)

#0503 Garnets
Heart on bird (SS)

#0575 Crispy leaf
Leaves (DLD)

Stems (BS)
Alphabet (BS)

#0154 Antique gold
Daisy centres (SS)
Bird beaks (BS)
Bird eyes (FK)
Bird crest feathers (BS with FK)

#0518 Dusty leaves
Dashed line under alphabet (RS)
Dashed line at top edge of design (RS)
Bird legs (BS)

Making the half-square triangle rows

7 You could make the half-square triangle (HST) units in the normal way, using a green and a burgundy 1⅜in (3.5cm) square, but with HSTs this small it's quite fiddly. If you want to use this two-at-once method then see Basic Techniques: Making Half-Square Triangles. I found it easier to use a paper template and foundation paper piecing technique instead. This method creates sixteen HSTs at once, each 1in (2.5cm) square, so you will need to copy the template in the Templates section carefully three times to create a total of thirty-six HSTs (see Tip). Place a green and a burgundy 5in (12.7cm) square right sides together (Fig 1). Place the paper template on top and pin in place (there will be some spare fabric around the edge). Sew along the dashed lines around each square, using a short stitch length (1.5mm). Cut the units apart on *all* of the solid lines (vertical, horizontal and diagonal). On each unit, press seams away from the paper and then, on the wrong side, fold the paper on the stitched seam and gently tear the paper away at an angle, from both sides of the stitched line.

Tip

If you plan to scan and print (or photocopy) the foundation paper piecing template, make sure when you print it that the 1in scaling square *is* 1in, and then you will know that the template is the correct size.

8 Take eighteen of the HSTs and sew them together to make a row, which should be 9½in (24.1cm) long once sewn. Make sure all of the triangles are facing in the right direction (Fig 2). Repeat with remaining HSTs so you have two rows.

Fig 2

1in
(2.5cm)

9½in
(24.1cm)

Fig 1

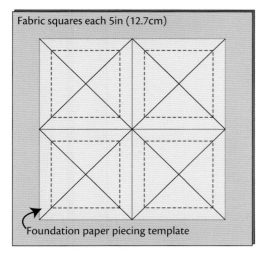

Fabric squares each 5in (12.7cm)

Foundation paper piecing template

Making the trim

9 Take the ¾in x 20in (2cm x 50.8cm) strip of burgundy swirl fabric and cut it into two strips each ¾in x 9½in (2cm x 24.1cm). Press the strips in half lengthways, wrong sides together.

Assembling the pillow front

10 Assemble the pillow as shown in Fig 3, sewing the pieces together in seven rows, as follows. Press seams away from the centre panel.

❀ One strip of blue stripe fabric 9½in x 2in (24.1cm x 5cm).

❀ One HST row.

❀ One strip of brown floral 9½in x 1in (24.1cm x 2.5cm).

❀ The centre panel.

❀ One strip of brown floral 9½in x 1in (24.1cm x 2.5cm).

❀ One HST row.

❀ One strip of blue stripe fabric 9½in x 2in (24.1cm x 5cm).

11 Place the folded trim along each side of the pillow centre, making sure the raw edges are aligned. Pin and then stitch in place with a very scant ¼in (6mm) seam allowance (Fig 4).

Fig 3

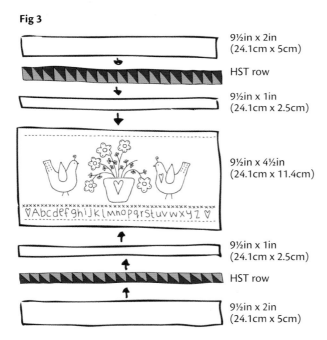

9½in x 2in (24.1cm x 5cm)

HST row

9½in x 1in (24.1cm x 2.5cm)

9½in x 4½in (24.1cm x 11.4cm)

9½in x 1in (24.1cm x 2.5cm)

HST row

9½in x 2in (24.1cm x 5cm)

Fig 4

Folded trim

Raw edge

Folded trim

12 Now sew a 4in x 9½in (10.2cm x 24.1cm) rectangle of blue swirl fabric to either side of the centre panel and press seams outwards (Fig 5). The pillow front should be 16½in x 9½in (42cm x 24.1cm) at this stage. Cut a piece of blue swirl print the same size as the front, for the back of the pillow.

Fig 5

Quilting and finishing

13 Bond a piece of lightweight fusible wadding (batting), such as Pellon, to the wrong side of the pillow front and also to the wrong side of the pillow back piece. Now quilt as desired. I used two strands of #0503 garnets and did some decorative running stitches about ¾in (2cm) outside the burgundy trim and outside the HST rows. Sew on the daisy button using matching thread.

14 With right sides together, pin and stitch the back and the front of the pillow together, leaving a small opening at the bottom (Fig 6). Clip the corners, turn through to the right side and press the seam. Fill the pillow with toy filling and then stitch the opening closed with ladder stitch and matching sewing thread.

Fig 6

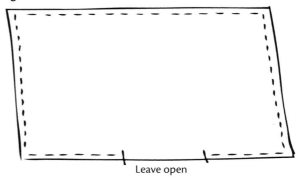

Leave open

Heart Mini Cushion

You will need…

❊ Cream print for stitchery background 3½in (8.9cm) square

❊ Blue floral fabric for backing 5in (12.7cm) square

❊ Four assorted prints for border 1½in x 5in (3.8cm x 12.7cm) strip of each

❊ Blue print for bird appliqué 2½in (6.4cm) square

❊ Mauve print for bird wing 1½in (3.8cm) square

❊ Fusible stitchery stabilizer 3½in (8.9cm) square (optional)

❊ Valdani stranded embroidery cotton (floss): #0503 garnets, #0575 crispy leaf, #0518 dusty leaves, #0511 black sea (see Materials & Equipment: Threads for DMC alternatives)

❊ Wadding (batting) 5in (12.7cm) square

❊ Fine-tipped fabric marking pen

❊ Toy filling for stuffing

Finished size
4½in (11.4cm) square approx.
Use ¼in (6mm) seams unless otherwise stated

Transferring the design

1 Copy the pattern from the Templates section. Using a light source, such as a light box/pad or window, place the cream background fabric centrally, right side up, over the pattern. Trace the stitchery lines onto the fabric using a fine-tipped fabric pen. Fuse the stitchery stabilizer to the back of the fabric (if using).

Working the appliqué

2 Using your favourite method of appliqué, prepare the bird and wing using the templates. Add a ¼in (6mm) seam allowance to the shapes for traditional needle-turn appliqué or, for fusible web, reverse the templates before use. I used needle-turn appliqué (see Basic Techniques: Needle-Turn Appliqué).

3 Position the bird in the centre of the heart. Glue baste or pin the shapes in place. Stitch them with a blind hem stitch, using a matching thread. Using a fine fabric marker, either freehand draw or trace the lines for the surface embroidery onto the appliqués.

−✕−✕−✕−✕−✕−✕−✕−✕−✕−✕−✕−✕−✕

Working the stitchery

4 Use two strands of Valdani thread. See Basic Techniques: Embroidery Stitches for how to work the stitches and Materials & Equipment: Threads for DMC alternatives. Stitches used are: backstitch (BS), satin stitch (SS), running stitch (RS), detached lazy daisy (DLD) and French knots (FK). When complete press carefully.

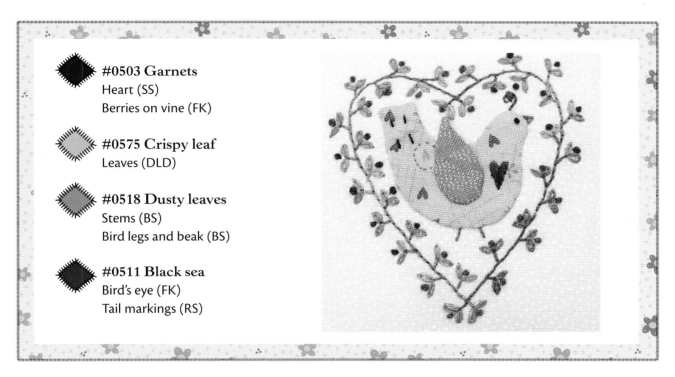

#0503 Garnets
Heart (SS)
Berries on vine (FK)

#0575 Crispy leaf
Leaves (DLD)

#0518 Dusty leaves
Stems (BS)
Bird legs and beak (BS)

#0511 Black sea
Bird's eye (FK)
Tail markings (RS)

Adding the border

5 From the four assorted prints cut the following.
❀ One 1¼in x 3½in (3.8cm x 8.9cm) – border 1.
❀ One 1¼in x 4¼in (3.8cm x 10.8cm) – border 2.
❀ One 1¼in x 4¼in (3.8cm x 10.8cm) – border 3.
❀ One 1¼in x 5in (3.8cm x 12.7cm) – border 4.
Sew the borders in place in the order shown in Fig 1.

Fig 1

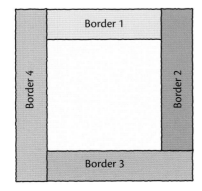

6 If desired, add a square of wadding (batting) behind the patchwork. Using two strands of #0503 garnets stranded cotton, quilt a running stitch line all around the border, about ¼in (6mm) away from the seam.

Making up

7 Pin the cushion front and back pieces right sides together and stitch together all round, leaving about 2in (5cm) unstitched at the bottom. Clip the corners, turn the cushion through to the right side and press the seam. Stuff firmly with toy filling, adding scented pot-pourri if you wish. Use ladder stitch and matching thread to sew the opening closed.

Daisy Chains

This quilt is full of interesting blocks and charming appliqué and the finished result is wonderful. It does take time to make and would suit a more experienced stitcher. I'm sure you will love it and give it pride of place in your home for many years to come. The quilt was made using my Pocketful of Daisies fabric collection, so details of those fabrics are included in the instructions, but the design could use other fabrics of your choice. This would be a great project to sew with friends, making the bands and borders on a month-by-month basis.

If you need a 'welcome to your new home' gift for a family member or friend, you are sure to have fun making just one house block for the Moonlight Cottage Wall Hanging. I made mine into an evening scene, displaying it as a wall hanging. It is hand quilted with big stitch quilting and embroidery cotton, to add texture and dimension.

Daisy Chain Cottages Quilt

You will need...

* Fabric A ¾yd (0.75m)
* Fabric B 1yd (1m)
* Fabric C ⅝yd (0.6m)
* Fabric D ½yd (0.5m)
* Fabric E ⅛yd (0.125m)
* Fabric F ¾yd (0.75m)
* Fabric G 1⅝yd (1.5m)
* Fabric H ½yd (0.5m)
* Fabric I 1⅞yd (1.75m) plus one fat quarter
* Fabric J 1yd (1m)
* Fabric K ⅞yd (0.8m)
* Fabric L 1⅜yd (1.25m)
* Fabric M ¾yd (0.75m)
* Fabric N ⅝yd (0.6m)
* Fabric O ⅝yd (0.6m)
* Fabric P ¼yd (0.25m)
* Fabric Q ¾yd (0.75m) plus one fat quarter
* Fabric R ½yd (0.5m)
* Fabric S ½yd (0.5m)
* Fabric T 1⅜yd (1.25m) plus one fat quarter
* Fabric U ¼yd (0.25m) plus one fat quarter
* Fabric V ½yd (0.5m)
* Fabric W ⅜yd (0.4m)
* Fabric X ¼yd (0.25m)
* Fabric Y ¾yd (0.75m)
* Assorted fabrics for appliqué – there are also lots of fabric off-cuts that can be used
* Wadding (batting) 76in x 88in (193cm x 224cm)
* Backing fabric 5yds (4.5m)
* Binding fabric ⅝yd (0.6m)
* Stranded embroidery cotton (floss): pale brown (bird), aged wine (bird), pale green, dark grey, medium green and brown (or other colours of your choice)

Finished size
70in x 82in (178cm x 208cm) approx
Use ¼in (6mm) seams unless otherwise stated
WOF = width of fabric
HST = half-square triangle

Fabric Choices and Quilt Layout

This quilt was made using my Pocketful of Daisies collection and the SKU (stock keeping unit) numbers are given in Fig 1. In the instructions the fabrics just use letters to identify them, so you can choose other fabrics if you prefer. Fabrics from my other ranges would also be suitable for this quilt. The quilt is made up of various bands and borders and the instructions start with the House Band, and work downwards. Fig 2 identifies the various parts of the quilt. There are numerous pieces of fabric needed for the quilt and it would be useful if you had some small clear folders or envelopes, labelled for the various bands and borders. Keep all fabric off-cuts as you go along.

Fig 1 Fabrics used
The code numbers for the fabrics in the
Pocketful of Daisies range are also given

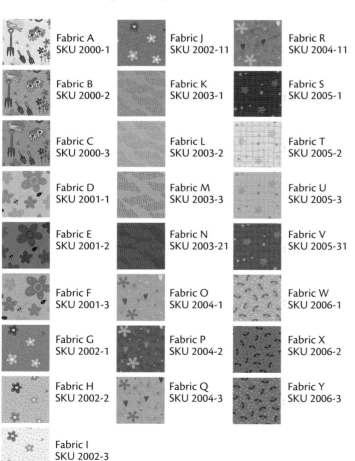

Fabric A SKU 2000-1	Fabric J SKU 2002-11	Fabric R SKU 2004-11
Fabric B SKU 2000-2	Fabric K SKU 2003-1	Fabric S SKU 2005-1
Fabric C SKU 2000-3	Fabric L SKU 2003-2	Fabric T SKU 2005-2
Fabric D SKU 2001-1	Fabric M SKU 2003-3	Fabric U SKU 2005-3
Fabric E SKU 2001-2	Fabric N SKU 2003-21	Fabric V SKU 2005-31
Fabric F SKU 2001-3	Fabric O SKU 2004-1	Fabric W SKU 2006-1
Fabric G SKU 2002-1	Fabric P SKU 2004-2	Fabric X SKU 2006-2
Fabric H SKU 2002-2	Fabric Q SKU 2004-3	Fabric Y SKU 2006-3
Fabric I SKU 2002-3		

−X−X− X−X−X− X−X−X− X−X−X− X−X−X

Fig 2 Quilt layout

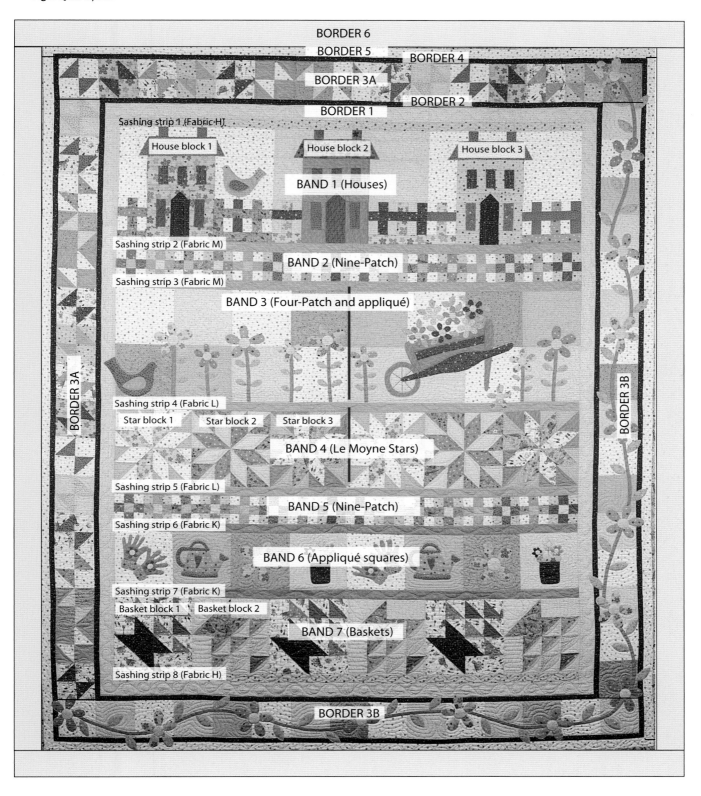

BORDER 6

BORDER 5

BORDER 4

BORDER 3A

BORDER 2

BORDER 1

Sashing strip 1 (Fabric H)

House block 1

House block 2

House block 3

BAND 1 (Houses)

Sashing strip 2 (Fabric M)

BAND 2 (Nine-Patch)

Sashing strip 3 (Fabric M)

BAND 3 (Four-Patch and appliqué)

BORDER 3A

BORDER 3B

Sashing strip 4 (Fabric L)

Star block 1   Star block 2   Star block 3

BAND 4 (Le Moyne Stars)

Sashing strip 5 (Fabric L)

BAND 5 (Nine-Patch)

Sashing strip 6 (Fabric K)

BAND 6 (Appliqué squares)

Sashing strip 7 (Fabric K)

Basket block 1   Basket block 2

BAND 7 (Baskets)

Sashing strip 8 (Fabric H)

BORDER 3B

Band 1 (House blocks)

This band consists of four house blocks. They are all made in the same way but use different fabrics. It is best to cut out and make one block at a time.

Cutting out House Block 1
Roof and Sky Section:

1 From Fabric I cut one strip 2½in (6.4cm) x WOF and sub-cut as follows.
❋ One 1½in x 3½in (3.8cm x 8.9cm).
❋ One 1½in x 4½in (3.8cm x 11.4cm).
❋ One 1½in x 7½in (3.8cm x 19cm).
❋ One 2½in x 5½in (6.4cm x 14cm).
❋ One 2½in (6.4cm) square.
Use the remainder to cut one 'M' and one 'O' shape using the templates provided.

2 From Fabric X cut one strip 2½in (6.4cm) x WOF and sub-cut as follows.
❋ Two 1½in (3.8cm) squares.
❋ One 2½in x 7½in (6.4cm x 19cm).
Use the remainder to cut one 'M' and one 'O' shape using the templates provided.

House and Sky Section:

3 From Fabric F cut one strip 1½in (3.8cm) x WOF and sub-cut as follows.
❋ Two 1½in (3.8cm) squares.
❋ Four 1½in x 2½in (3.8cm x 6.4cm).
❋ Two 1½in x 3in (3.8cm x 7.6cm).
❋ One 1in x 7½in (2.5cm x 19cm).
❋ One 1½in x 7½in (3.8cm x 19cm).

4 From Fabric I cut one strip 5in x WOF and sub-cut as follows.
❋ One 5in x 3½in (12.7cm x 8.9cm).
❋ One 5in x 6½in (12.7cm x 16.5cm).

5 From Fabric P cut one strip 1½in (3.8cm) x WOF. Sub-cut into three 1½in x 2½in (3.8cm x 6.4cm).

6 From Fabric S cut one strip 2½in (6.4cm) x WOF and sub-cut one 2½in x 1½in (6.4cm x 3.8cm).

House and Fence Section:

7 From Fabric C cut one strip 1½in (3.8cm) x WOF and sub-cut as follows.
❋ Three 1½in (3.8cm) squares.
❋ Three 1½in x 2in (3.8cm x 5cm).
❋ Two 1½in x 3½in (3.8cm x 8.9cm).
❋ Two 1½in x 6½in (3.8cm x 16.5cm).

8 From Fabric F cut one strip 2in (5cm) x WOF and sub-cut as follows.
❋ Two 1in x 3½in (2.5cm x 8.9cm).
❋ Two 1½in x 3½in (3.8cm x 8.9cm).
❋ Two 2in x 3in (5cm x 7.6cm).

9 From the remainder of Fabric I sub-cut the following.
❋ Five 1½in (3.8cm) squares.
❋ Five 1½in x 2in (3.8cm x 5cm).

10 From Fabric J cut one strip 1½in (3.8cm) x WOF. Sub-cut one 1½in x 3½in (3.8cm x 8.9cm).

11 From Fabric N cut one strip 1½in (3.8cm) x WOF and sub-cut as follows.
❀ One 1½in (3.8cm) square.
❀ One 1½in x 2in (3.8cm x 5cm).
❀ Two 1½in x 3½in (3.8cm x 8.9cm).

12 From the remainder of Fabric S cut one 2½in x 5in (6.4cm x 12.7cm).

13 For the appliqué bird use the template to cut a body from Fabric L and wing from Fabric Y.

Cutting out House Block 2
Roof and Sky Section:
1 From Fabric T cut one strip 2½in (6.4cm) x WOF and sub-cut as follows.
❀ One 1½in x 3½in (3.8cm x 8.9cm).
❀ One 1½in x 4½in (3.8cm x 11.4cm).
❀ One 1½in x 7½in (3.8cm x 19cm).
❀ One 2½in x 5½in (6.4cm x 14cm).
❀ One 2½in (6.4cm) square.

Use the remainder to cut one 'M' and one 'O' shape using the templates provided.

2 From Fabric E cut one strip 2½in (6.4cm) x WOF and sub-cut as follows.
❀ Two 1½in (3.8cm) squares.
❀ One 2½in x 7½in (6.4cm x 19cm).

Use the remainder to cut one 'M' shape and one 'O' shape using the templates provided.

House and Sky Section:
3 From Fabric K cut one strip 1½in (3.8cm) x WOF and sub-cut as follows.
❀ Two 1½in (3.8cm) squares.
❀ Four 1½in x 2½in (3.8cm x 6.4cm).
❀ Two 1½in x 3in (3.8cm x 7.6cm).
❀ One 1½in x 7½in (3.8cm x 19cm).
❀ One 1in x 7½in (2.5cm x 19cm).

4 From Fabric T cut one strip 5in (12.7cm) x WOF and sub-cut as follows.
❀ One 5in x 3½in (12.7cm x 8.9cm).
❀ One 5in x 6½in (12.7cm x 16.5cm).

Use the remainder for the house and the fence.

5 From Fabric N cut one strip 2½in (6.4cm) x WOF and sub-cut into three 1½in x 2½in (3.8cm x 6.4cm). Keep the remainder for a door piece for the house and fence section.

House and Fence Section:
6 From the remainder of Fabric T cut the following pieces.
❀ Five 1½in (3.8cm) squares.
❀ Five 1½in x 2in (3.8cm x 5cm).

7 From the remainder of Fabric N cut one 2½in x 5in (6.4cm x 12.7cm).

8 From Fabric K cut one strip 2in (5cm) x WOF and sub-cut as follows.
❀ Two 1in x 3½in (2.5cm x 8.9cm).
❀ Two 1½in x 3½in (3.8cm x 8.9cm).
❀ Two 2in x 3in (5cm x 7.6cm).

9 From Fabric D cut one strip 1½in (3.8cm) x WOF and sub-cut as follows.
❀ Two 1½in (3.8cm) squares.
❀ Two 1½in x 2in (3.8cm x 5cm).
❀ One 1½in x 3½in (3.8cm x 8.9cm).
❀ One 1½in x 6½in (3.8cm x 16.5cm).

10 From Fabric P cut one strip 1½in (3.8cm) x WOF and sub-cut as follows.
❀ Two 1½in (3.8cm) squares.
❀ Two 1½in x 2in (3.8cm x 5cm).
❀ One 1½in x 3½in (3.8cm x 8.9cm).
❀ One 1½in x 6½in (3.8cm x 16.5cm).

11 From Fabric X cut one strip 1½in (3.8cm) x WOF and sub-cut into two 1½in x 3½in (3.8cm x 8.9cm).

Cutting out House Block 3
Roof and Sky Section:
1 From Fabric I cut one strip 2½in (6.4cm) x WOF and sub-cut as follows.
❀ One 1½in x 3½in (3.8cm x 8.9cm).
❀ One 1½in x 4½in (3.8cm x 11.4cm).
❀ One 1½in x 7½in (3.8cm x 19cm).
❀ One 2½in x 5½in (6.4cm x 14cm).
❀ One 2½in (6.4cm) square.

Use the remainder to cut one 'M' and one 'O' shape using the templates provided.

2 From Fabric Y cut one strip 2½in (6.4cm) x WOF and sub-cut as follows.
❀ Two 1½in (3.8cm) squares.
❀ One 2½in x 7½in (6.4cm x 19cm).

Use the remainder to cut one 'M' and one 'O' shape using the templates provided.

House and Sky Section:
3 From Fabric H cut one strip 1½in (3.8cm) x WOF and sub-cut as follows.
❀ Two 1½in (3.8cm) squares.
❀ Four 1½in x 2½in (3.8cm x 6.4cm).
❀ Two 1½in x 3in (3.8cm x 7.6cm).
❀ One 1½in x 7½in (3.8cm x 19cm).
❀ One 1in x 7½in (2.5cm x 19cm).

4 From Fabric I cut one strip 5in (12.7cm) x WOF and sub-cut as follows.
❀ One 5in x 3½in (12.7cm x 8.9cm).
❀ One 5in x 6½in (12.7cm x 16.5cm).

Use the remainder to cut pieces for house and fence.

5 From Fabric V cut one strip 1½in (3.8cm) x WOF and sub-cut into three pieces 1½in x 2½in.

6 From Fabric S cut one strip 2½in (6.4cm) x WOF and sub-cut one 2½in x 1½in (6.4cm x 3.8cm). Keep the remainder for the house and fence.

House and Fence Section:
7 From the remainder of Fabric I cut the following pieces.
❀ Five 1½in (3.8cm) squares.
❀ Five 1½in x 2in (3.8cm x 5cm).

8 From Fabric H cut one strip 2in x WOF and sub-cut as follows.
❀ Two 1in x 3½in (2.5cm x 8.9cm).
❀ Two 1½in x 3½in (3.8cm x 8.9cm).
❀ Two 2in x 3in (5cm x 7.6cm).

9 From the remainder of Fabric S cut one 2½in x 5in (6.4cm x 12.7cm).

10 From Fabric R cut one strip 1½in (3.8cm) x WOF and sub-cut into two 1½in x 3½in (3.8cm x 8.9cm).

11 From Fabric G cut one strip 1½in (3.8cm) x WOF and sub-cut as follows.
❀ One 1½in (3.8cm) square.
❀ One 1½in x 2in (3.8cm x 5cm).
❀ Two 1½in x 6½in (3.8cm x 16.5cm).

12 From Fabric X cut one strip 1½in (3.8cm) x WOF and sub-cut as follows.
❀ Two 1½in (3.8cm) squares.
❀ Two 1½in x 2in (3.8cm x 5cm).
❀ One 1½in x 3½in (3.8cm x 8.9cm).
❀ One 1½in x 6½in (3.8cm x 16.5cm).

13 From Fabric D cut one strip 1½in (3.8cm) x WOF and sub-cut as follows.
❀ One 1½in (3.8cm) square.
❀ One 1½in x 2in (3.8cm x 5cm).
❀ One 1½in x 3½in (3.8cm x 8.9cm).

Making a House block

House block 1 is used as an example, so follow these instructions when making House Blocks 2 and 3, but changing fabrics as noted in the cutting lists.

Roof and Sky

 Arrange and sew together into a row (as shown in Fig 3), two 1½in (3.8cm) Fabric X squares, one 1½in x 3½in (3.8cm x 8.9cm) Fabric I rectangle, one 1½in x 4½in (3.8cm x 11.4cm) Fabric I rectangle, and one 1½in x 7½in (3.8cm x 19cm) Fabric I rectangle.

Fig 3

 Sew together the template pieces of Fabric X and Fabric I ('M' and 'O') to make two half-rectangle units (Fig 4).

Fig 4

3 Arrange and sew together into a row (as Fig 5) two half-rectangle units, one 2½in (6.4cm) Fabric I square, one 2½in x 5½in (6.4cm x 14cm) Fabric I rectangle and one 2½in x 7½in (6.4cm x 19cm) Fabric X rectangle.

Fig 5

4 Sew the rows together to complete the roof and sky section (Fig 6). Check the sewn unit measures 3½in x 16½in (8.9cm x 41.9cm).

Fig 6

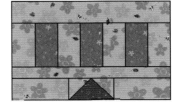

House and Sky

5 To create the top of the door, draw a diagonal line on the wrong side of a 1½in (3.8cm) Fabric F square. Place the square, right sides together, at a corner of one 1½in x 2½in (3.8cm x 6.4cm) Fabric S rectangle. Sew on the drawn line. Trim ¼in (6mm) away from the line and press open. Repeat with another Fabric F square on the opposite side of the same Fabric S rectangle to complete the flying geese unit (Fig 7). Sew a 1½in x 3in (3.8cm x 7.6cm) Fabric F rectangle to each short side of the flying geese unit.

Fig 7

6 Sew a 1in x 7½in (2.5cm x 19cm) Fabric F rectangle to the top of this unit (Fig 8).

Fig 8

7 For the top windows, take four 1½in x 2½in (3.8cm x 6.4cm) Fabric F rectangles and three 1½in x 2½in (3.8cm x 6.4cm) Fabric P rectangles. Arrange them alternately as Fig 9. Sew together and add to the top of the unit made in the last step.

Fig 9

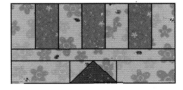

8 Sew one 1½in x 7½in (3.8cm x 19cm) Fabric F rectangle to the top of this unit (Fig 10).

Fig 10

9 Complete this unit by sewing a 5in x 3½in (12.7cm x 8.9cm) Fabric I rectangle to the left side of the unit and a 5in x 6½in (12.7cm x 16.5cm) Fabric I rectangle to the right side of the unit (Fig 11).

Fig 11

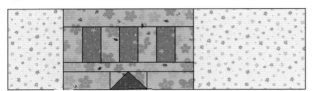

House and Fence

10 Sew the fence left-hand side as follows. Sew one 1½in (3.8cm) Fabric C square between two 1½in (3.8cm) Fabric I squares. Sew one 1½in x 2in (3.8cm x 5cm) Fabric C rectangle between two 1½in x 2in (3.8cm x 5cm) Fabric I rectangles. Sew one 1½in x 3½in (3.8cm x 8.9cm) Fabric J rectangle between these two sewn units, as in Fig 12. Sew one 1½in x 3½in (3.8cm x 8.9cm) Fabric C rectangle to the bottom of the unit to complete the left-hand fence unit.

Fig 12

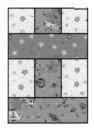

11 For the lower windows, sew one 1½in x 3½in (3.8cm x 8.9cm) Fabric F rectangle to one 1½in x 3½in (3.8cm x 8.9cm) Fabric N rectangle (Fig 13). Add one 1in x 3½in (2.5cm x 8.9cm) Fabric F rectangle to the right-hand side. Add one 2in x 3in (5cm x 7.6cm) Fabric F rectangle to the bottom of sewn unit. Repeat to make a total of two units (Fig 14).

Fig 13    **Fig 14**

12 Take the two sewn window units and sew one 2½in x 5in (6.4cm x 12.7cm) Fabric S rectangle between them for the door (Fig 15).

Fig 15

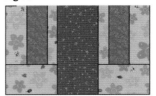

13 Sew the fence right-hand side as follows. Following Fig 16, sew together the following 1½in (3.8cm) squares – Fabric I, C, I, N, I, C. Arrange and sew together the following 1½in x 2in (3.8cm x 5cm) rectangles – Fabric I, C, I, N, I, C. Sew a 1½in x 6½in (3.8cm x 16.5cm) Fabric C rectangle between the squares unit and the rectangles unit. Sew a 1½in x 6½in (3.8cm x 16.5cm) Fabric C rectangle to the bottom to complete the right-hand fence unit.

Fig 16

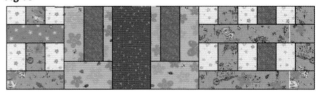

14 Sew the fence and door units together to complete the house and fence section. Sew all the sections together to complete House Block 1 (Fig 17). Check the unit measures 12½in x 16½in (31.8cm x 41.9cm).

Fig 17

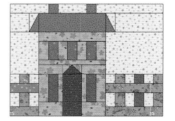

15 Repeat the process in Steps 1–14 to make House Block 2 and then House 3 using the correct fabric pieces for those blocks (Fig 18). Sew the house blocks together to complete the band (Fig 19).

Fig 18

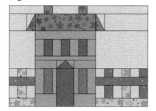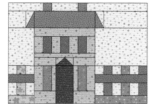

Fig 19

Adding the appliqué

16 Using the templates provided, prepare the bird and wing shapes for needle-turn appliqué (see Basic Techniques: Needle-Turn Appliqué) with a seam allowance of ⅛in–¼in (3mm–6mm). Place the bird on the right-hand fence of House block 1 and sew into place. Using two strands of brown embroidery cotton (floss), embroider the bird's legs and beak in backstitch and three lines of running stitch on the tail. Add the eye with a French knot in wine and outline the wing with running stitches.

Band 2 (Nine-Patch) and Band 3 (Four-Patch and Appliqué)

Band 2 is sixteen nine-patch units sewn together. Band 3 is made up of large squares (essentially four four-patch units), which are then embellished with appliqué. Note that Band 3 is made in two stages, a left and a right half, each with eight 6½in (16.5cm) squares. Keep all fabric off-cuts to use later.

Cutting out

1 From Fabric I, cut one strip 6½in (16.5cm) x WOF. Sub-cut the following.
* Three 6½in (16.5cm) squares.
* Thirty-two 1½in (3.8cm) squares.

2 From Fabric Q, cut one strip 6½in (16.5cm) x WOF. Sub-cut two 6½in (16.5cm) squares.

3 From Fabric T, cut one strip 6½in (16.5cm) x WOF. Sub-cut the following.
* Two 6½in (16.5cm) squares.
* Eight 1½in (3.8cm) squares.

4 From Fabric U, cut one strip 6½in (16.5cm) x WOF. Sub-cut the following.
* One 6½in (16.5cm) square.
* Eight 1½in (3.8cm) squares.

5 From Fabrics C, G, J, N, R and W cut one strip 1½in (3.8cm) x WOF. Sub-cut each strip into eight 1½in (3.8cm) squares.

6 From Fabric H, cut two strips 1½in (3.8cm) x WOF. Sub-cut thirty-two 1½in (3.8cm) squares.

7 From Fabric L, cut one strip 1½in (3.8cm) x WOF. Sub-cut sixteen 1½in (3.8cm) squares.

Making Band 2

This row consists of two groups of eight nine-patch units. The following instructions use the Fabric U, Fabric R and Fabric I example.

1 Take nine 1½in (3.8cm) squares and sew them together into three rows each with three squares (Fig 20). Press the seams of row 2 in the opposite direction to rows 1 and 3. Sew the rows together to complete a nine-patch unit.

Fig 20

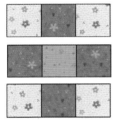

2 Refer to Fig 21 and make a total of two units for each colourway. Sew the units together to complete one group. Make a total of two groups. Sew the groups together to complete the band.

Fig 21

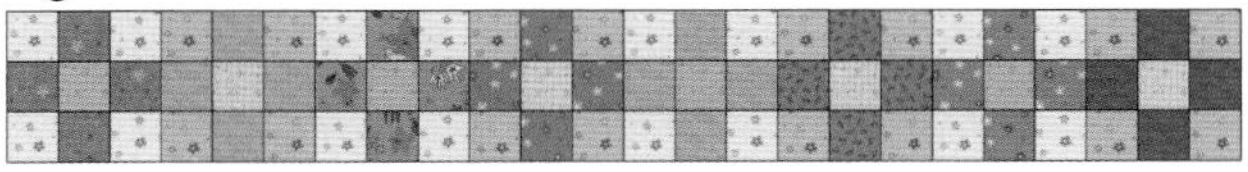

Making Band 3 (left half)

This part of Band 3 consists of eight 6½in (16.5cm) squares, sewn together in two rows. The pieced section is then embellished with five appliquéd flowers. Note that the appliqué bird is added later, when Border 1 is sewn in place.

3 Arrange and sew the 6½in (16.5cm) squares into rows as follows.

❀ Row 1 – Fabric I, Fabric T, Fabric I, Fabric Q (Fig 22).

❀ Row 2 – Fabric Q, Fabric U, Fabric T, Fabric I (Fig 23).

Press the seams of one row in one direction and in the opposite direction for the second row. Sew the two rows together to finish the piecing.

Fig 22

Fig 23

Adding the appliqué

4 Prepare the following appliqué shapes: three large flowers (Fabrics D, G and F), three large flower centres (Fabric T), twelve large leaves (Fabric O), two small flowers (Fabrics D and J), two small flower centres (Fabric T), eight small leaves (Fabric O), eight flower stems, each finishing ¼in (6mm) wide (Fabric F). Make long lengths for stems from bias-cut strips ¾in (2cm) wide. Fold in and press a ¼in (6mm) seam down each long edge (or use a bias maker tool). You can then cut the lengths required for each flower.

5 Add the appliqué pieces to the left half of Band 3 using the method of your choice (Fig 24).

Fig 24

Making Band 3 (right half) and Band 5 (Nine-Patch)

This right-hand half of Band 3 consists of eight 6½in (16.5cm) squares, sewn together in two rows (as for the left side). The pieced section is then embellished with an appliquéd wheelbarrow of flowers and four flowers. Band 5 is also made at this time, which is a repeat of the Nine-Patch blocks made for Band 2.

Cutting out

1 From Fabric I, cut one strip 6½in (16.5cm) x WOF. Sub-cut the following.
❀ Three 6½in (16.5cm) squares.
❀ Thirty-two 1½in (3.8cm) squares.

2 From the remainder of Fabric Q sub-cut one 6½in (16.5cm) square.

3 From the remainder of Fabric T sub-cut the following.
❀ Three 6½in (16.5cm) squares.
❀ Eight 1½in (3.8cm) squares.

4 From the remainder of Fabric U sub-cut the following.
❀ Two 6½in (16.5cm) squares.
❀ Eight 1½in (3.8cm) squares.

5 From the remainder of Fabrics C, G and J sub-cut from each eight 1½in (3.8cm) squares.

6 From the remainder of Fabric H sub-cut thirty-two 1½in (3.8cm) squares.

7 From Fabric L, cut three strips 1½in (3.8cm) x WOF and sub-cut sixteen 1½in (3.8cm) squares for nine-patch units. Join the remaining two strips and sub-cut one sashing strip 1½in x 48½in (3.8cm x 123.2cm).

8 From the remainder of Fabric N and Fabric R sub-cut from each eight 1½in (3.8cm) squares.

9 From the remainder of Fabric W sub-cut eight 1½in (3.8cm) squares.

Making Band 3 (right half)

1 Arrange and sew together the 6½in (16.5cm) squares into rows as follows. Row 1 – Fabrics U, T, I, U (Fig 25). Row 2 – Fabrics T, I, Q, T (Fig 26). Sew the rows together to complete this half of Band 3.

Fig 25

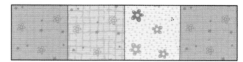

Fig 26

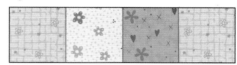

2 Sew both halves of Band 3 together. Add the Fabric L sashing strip to the bottom of the band (Fig 27).

Fig 27

Adding the appliqué

3 For this right-hand side of Band 3 prepare one large flower (Fabric G), one large flower centre (Fabric T), three small flowers (Fabrics D, F and G), three small flower centres (Fabric T), four large leaves (Fabric O), eight small leaves (Fabric O), two wheelbarrow flowers (Fabric J), two wheelbarrow flowers (Fabric V), two wheelbarrow flowers (Fabric W), sixteen wheelbarrow leaves (Fabric O), wheelbarrow cart pieces (Fabric K), wheelbarrow cart pieces (Fabric P), three flower stems (Fabric F) to finish at ¼in (6mm) wide.

4 Add the appliqué pieces to the right half of Band 3 using the method of your choice, using Fig 28 as a placement guide. Embellish by embroidering leaf veins using pale green cotton (floss), and dark grey for the wood grain on the wheelbarrow frame at the base and the spokes of the wheel.

Fig 28

Making Band 5 (Nine-Patch)

5 This band is made in the same way as Band 2. Take the 144 1½in (3.8cm) squares cut earlier and follow the previous instructions in Making Band 2 (Steps 1 and 2) for making sixteen nine-patch units. Sew the units together to complete the band (Fig 29).

Fig 29

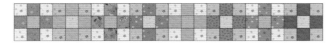

Band 4 (Le Moyne Stars) and Band 6 (Appliqué Squares)

This section describes how to make the Le Moyne Star blocks for Band 4 and also two of the appliqué squares for Band 6 (the garden glove and watering can).

Cutting out

1 Cut the following pieces for the Le Moyne Stars using the templates provided. There are six stars in the band, two of three different colourways.
❋ Eight 'A' shapes from each of Fabrics A, B, D, I, J and T.
❋ Eight 'B' shapes from each of Fabrics C, I, K and T.
❋ Eight 'C' shapes from each of Fabrics C, I, K and T.
❋ Sixteen 'B' shapes from Fabric U.
❋ Sixteen 'C' shapes from Fabric U.

2 For the appliquéd squares in Band 6, cut two 6½in (16.5cm) squares each from Fabric I and Fabric U. This is for half of the band: the remaining squares will be cut in the next section.

Making the Le Moyne Star blocks

1 In Band 4 there are six Le Moyne Star blocks, in three different colourways. The following instructions describe the far left block as an example. Using the Le Moyne Star templates 'A', 'B' and 'C' and an English paper piecing technique, piece together one quadrant unit as shown in Fig 30, using Fabrics D, I and U. See Basic Techniques: English Paper Piecing. Repeat to make a total of four quadrants.

Fig 30

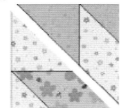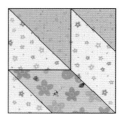

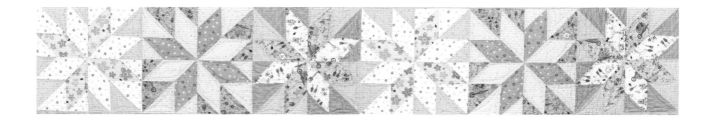

2 Following Fig 31, sew four quadrants together to complete one block. Check the block is 8½in (21.6cm) square.

Fig 31

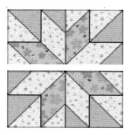 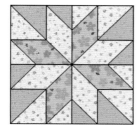

3 Make a total of two blocks for each of the colourways shown in Fig 32, so you have a total of six stars. Arrange and sew the blocks together to complete the band (Fig 33).

Fig 32

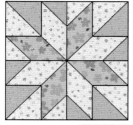 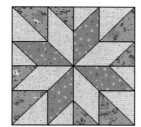

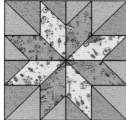

Fig 33

Adding the appliqués for Band 6

4 Using the templates provided, cut two of each shape as follows: garden glove (Fabric K), glove cuff (Fabric G), glove flower (Fabric M), watering can handle, lid, base and spout (Fabric Y), watering can body (Fabric G), watering can heart (Fabric N), flower centre (Fabric T).

5 Prepare the appliqué pieces in the method of your choice – I used needle-turn appliqué. Note that only the gloves and watering can squares are made in this section. Using Fig 34 as a guide, arrange and sew the appliqué pieces in place on the Fabric I and Fabric U 6½in (16.5cm) squares. Sew the squares together. Make two units like this and set aside for the moment.

Fig 34

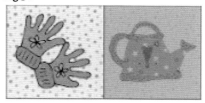

Band 6 (Appliqué Squares) and Band 7 (Basket Blocks)

This section describes how to make the remaining two appliqué squares (flower and flower in pot) for Band 6 and also the basket blocks for Band 7.

Cutting out

1 From Fabric H, Fabric K and Fabric M cut three 1½in (3.8cm) x WOF strips for sashing. Join the strips from the same fabric and sub-cut two strips 1½in x 48½in (3.8cm x 123.2cm).

2 From Fabric L cut two 1½in (3.8cm) x WOF strips for sashing. Join the strips and sub-cut one 1½in x 48½in (3.8cm x 123.2cm). Note that one sashing strip has already been added to the bottom of Band 3.

3 From Fabric A and Fabric T cut the following (see also Fig 44).
❀ One strip 2½in (6.4cm) x WOF. Sub-cut three 2½in (6.4cm) squares and six 2½in x 4½in (6.4cm x 11.4cm).
❀ Two strips 2⅞in (7.3cm) x WOF. Sub-cut fifteen 2⅞in (7.3cm) squares. Sub-cut three 2⅞in (7.3cm) squares once diagonally to yield six triangles.

4 From Fabric S and Fabric C cut one strip 3in (7.6cm) x WOF. Sub-cut into three 2½in (6.4cm) squares and six 2⅞in (7.3cm) squares.

5 From Fabric J and Fabric G cut one strip 2⅞in (7.3cm) x WOF. Sub-cut five 2⅞in (7.3cm) squares. Cut two 2⅞in (7.3cm) squares once diagonally to yield four triangles.

6 From Fabrics N and Fabric W cut one strip 2⅞in (7.3cm) x WOF. Sub-cut three 2⅞in (7.3cm) squares.

7 From Fabric X and Fabric R cut one strip 2⅞in (7.3cm) x WOF. Sub-cut two 2⅞in (7.3cm) squares. Cut two 2⅞in (7.3cm) squares once diagonally to yield four triangles.

8 For the appliqué background blocks, cut two 6½in (16.5cm) squares from Fabric Q and cut two 6½in (16.5cm) squares Fabric T.

Adding the appliqués to Band 6

1 Using the templates provided, cut two each of the flower pot flowers (Fabric J, Fabric V, Fabric W), six flower pot flower centres (Fabric T), two pot rims (Fabric F), two pot bases (Fabric S), two large flowers (Fabric F) and two large flower centres (Fabric T).

2 Prepare the appliqué pieces in the method of your choice – I used needle-turn appliqué. Using Fig 35 as a guide, arrange and sew the appliqués in place on the Fabric Q and Fabric T 6½in (16.5cm) squares. Embroider the stems and leaves in black stranded cotton. Sew the squares together. Make two units like this.

Fig 35

3 Take the eight appliqué blocks made previously and sew them into a row (Fig 36).

Fig 36

Making the Basket Blocks

4 In Band 6 there are six basket blocks, in two different colourways. Some of the HSTs are made in pairs from squares, while some are sewn from two individual triangles. These instructions describe the far left block as an example. Draw a diagonal line on the wrong side of one 2⅞in (7.3cm) Fabric A square. Place the square, right sides together, on one 2⅞in (7.3cm) Fabric S square. Sew ¼in (6mm) away from, and on both sides of the drawn line. Cut along the drawn line. Open and press to yield two HST units (Fig 37). Check the units are 2½in (6.4cm) square.

Fig 37

5 Repeat this process to make further HST units – four HSTs using Fabrics A and S, two HSTs using Fabrics A and J and two HSTs using Fabrics A and N.

6 Sew the previously cut triangles together to make one Fabric A/Fabric J HST unit and one Fabric A/ Fabric X HST unit. Now arrange and sew the HST units together into rows (Fig 38).

Fig 38

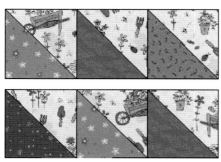

7 Sew the rows together, as shown. And add one 2½in x 4½in (6.4cm x 11.4cm) Fabric A rectangle to the left of the sewn unit to complete the top half of the basket block (Fig 39).

Fig 39

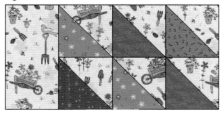

8 Arrange and sew together one 2½in (6.4cm) Fabric S square and three HST units into a row (Fig 40).

Fig 40

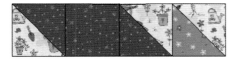

9 Arrange and sew together one HST unit, one 2½in (6.4cm) Fabric A square and one 2½in x 4½in (6.4cm x 11.4cm) Fabric A rectangle into a row (Fig 41).

Fig 41

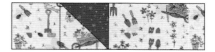

10 Sew the rows together to complete the bottom half of the basket block (Fig 42). Sew the top and bottom halves together to complete one block (Fig 43). Check it is 8½in (21.6cm) square.

Fig 42

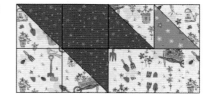

Fig 43

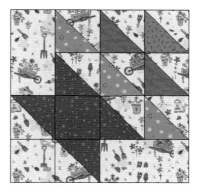

11 Repeat to make a total of three blocks in each of the colourways shown in Fig 44.

Fig 44

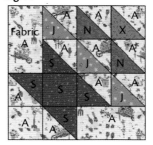
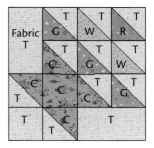

12 Arrange and sew blocks together into a row (Fig 45). The row should measure 8½in x 48½in (21.6 x 123.2cm).

Fig 45

Assembling the quilt centre

13 Referring to the quilt layout diagram (Fig 2), you can now sew the bands you have made together, with sashing strips between (see also Fig 46). Sew together from the top down, pressing the seams towards the sashing strips.

Fig 46

Adding the Quilt Borders

Once all of the bands and sashing strips are sewn together you can begin to add the quilt borders. There are six borders altogether. All of them are plain strips of fabric, with the exception of Border 3, which is pieced in two different patterns (Border 3A and 3B). The bird appliqué for Band 3 is also added at this stage. See Fig 2 for the labelled parts of the quilt.

Cutting out

1 From Fabric A, cut the following for the pieced blocks in Border 3A.

❋ Two strips 2½in (6.4cm) x WOF. Sub-cut eighteen 2½in (6.4cm) squares.

❋ One strip 2⅞in (7.3cm) x WOF. Sub-cut into nine 2⅞in (7.3cm) squares.

2 From Fabric B for final Border 6 cut eight strips each 4in (10.2cm) x WOF. Join the strips and sub-cut two strips 4in x 70½in (10.2cm x 179cm) and two strips 4in x 75½in (10.2cm x 191.8cm).

3 From Fabric F cut for the pieced blocks in Border 3A one strip 2⅞in (7.3cm) x WOF. Sub-cut six 2½in (6.4cm) squares and three 2⅞in (7.3cm) squares.

4 From Fabric G cut for the pieced blocks in Border 3A one strip 2⅞in (7.3cm) x WOF. Sub-cut three 2⅞in (7.3cm) squares.

5 From Fabric H cut for the pieced blocks in Border 3A one strip 2⅞in (7.3cm) x WOF. Sub-cut six 2½in (6.4cm) squares and three 2⅞in (7.3cm) squares.

6 From Fabric I cut the following for the pieced blocks in Border 3A.

❋ Two strips 2½in (6.4cm) x WOF. Sub-cut twelve 2½in (6.4cm) squares.

❋ One strip 2⅞in (7.3cm) x WOF. Sub-cut nine 2⅞in (7.3cm) squares.

7 From Fabric I cut for the blocks in Border 3B two strips 4½in (11.4cm) x WOF. Sub-cut twelve 4½in (11.4cm) squares.

8 From Fabric I cut for Border 5 eight strips 1½in (3.8cm) x WOF. Join the strips and sub-cut two strips 1½in x 63½in and two 1½in x 73½in.

9 From Fabric L cut for the pieced blocks in Border 3A one strip 2⅞in (7.3cm) x WOF. Sub-cut three 2⅞in (7.3cm) squares.

10 From Fabric M cut for the pieced blocks in Border 3A one strip 2⅞in (7.3cm) x WOF. Sub-cut six 2⅞in (7.3cm) squares and six 2½in (6.4cm) squares.

11 From Fabric O cut for the pieced blocks in Border 3A one strip 2⅞in (7.3cm) x WOF. Sub-cut six 2½in (6.4cm) squares and three 2⅞in (7.3cm) squares.

12 From Fabric P cut for the pieced blocks in Border 3A one strip 2⅞in (7.3cm) x WOF. Sub-cut three 2⅞in (7.3cm) squares.

13 From Fabric Q cut for the pieced blocks in Border 3B one strip 4½in (11.4cm) x WOF. Sub-cut four 4½in (11.4cm) squares.

14 From Fabric S cut for Border 2 and Border 4, fourteen strips 1in (2.5cm) x WOF. Join the strips together and sub-cut the following.
✴ Two 1in x 52½in (2.5cm x 133.4cm) (Border 2).
✴ Two 1in x 63½in (2.5cm x 161.3cm) (Border 2).
✴ Two 1in x 61½in (2.5cm x 156.2cm) (Border 4).
✴ Two 1in x 72½in (2.5cm x 184.2cm) (Border 4).

15 From Fabric T cut for the pieced blocks in Border 3A, one strip 2⅞in (7.3cm) x WOF. Sub-cut six 2½in (6.4cm) squares and six 2⅞in (7.3cm) squares.

16 From Fabric T cut for Border 1, six 2in x WOF strips. Join the strips together and then sub-cut the following.
✴ Two 2in x 51½in (5cm x 130.8cm).
✴ Two 2in x 60½in (5cm x 153.7cm).

17 From Fabric T cut for the blocks in Border 3B, two strips 4½in (11.4cm) x WOF. Sub-cut twelve 4½in (11.4cm) squares.

18 From Fabric U cut for the blocks in Border 3B, one strip 4½in (11.4cm) x WOF. Sub-cut four 4½in (11.4cm) squares.

19 From Fabric V cut for the pieced blocks in Border 3A, one strip 2⅞in (7.3cm) x WOF. Sub-cut three 2⅞in (7.3cm) squares.

20 From Fabric W cut for the pieced blocks in Border 3A, one strip 2⅞in (7.3cm) x WOF. Sub-cut three 2⅞in (7.3cm) squares.

21 From Fabric X cut for the pieced blocks in Border 3A, one strip 2⅞in (7.3cm) x WOF. Sub-cut three 2⅞in (7.3cm) squares.

22 From Fabric Y cut for the pieced blocks in Border 3A, one strip 2⅞in (7.3cm) x WOF. Sub-cut three 2⅞in (7.3cm) squares.

Adding Border 1

1 Sew two 2in x 60½in (5cm x 153.7cm) Fabric T strips to the long sides of the quilt (Fig 47). Sew two 2in x 51½in (5cm x 130.8cm) Fabric T strips to the top and bottom of the quilt.

Adding Border 2

2 Sew two 1in x 63½in (2.5cm x 161.3cm) Fabric S strips to the sides of the quilt. Sew two 1in x 52½in (2.5cm x 133.4cm) Fabric S strips to the top and bottom of the quilt (Fig 27).

Fig 47

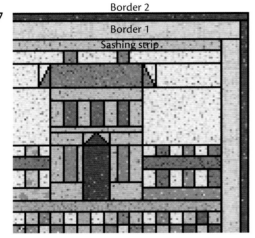

Making the Border 3A blocks

This pieced border is made up of Border 3A and 3B. Border 3A (one long and one shorter) is made up of four-patch blocks, with each block made up of two 2½in (6.4cm) squares and two HST units. The pieced blocks in Border 3A are made in groups of ten (ten colourway combinations repeated three times). Border 3B (one long and one short) is made up of 4½in (11.4cm) squares, with appliqué added after piecing.

3 The top right block is used as an example. Draw a diagonal line on the wrong side of one 2⅞in (7.3cm) Fabric H square. Place the square, right sides together, on one 2⅞in (7.3cm) Fabric L square. Sew ¼in (6mm) away from the drawn line, on both sides. Cut along the drawn line and press open to yield two HST units. Check each unit is 2½in (6.4cm) square.

4 Repeat this process to make six HST units of each of the following combinations:

❀ Fabric H/Fabric L, Fabric M/Fabric A.
❀ Fabric F/Fabric V, Fabric I/Fabric X.
❀ Fabric T/Fabric W, Fabric Y/Fabric A.
❀ Fabric I/Fabric G, Fabric O/Fabric T.
❀ Fabric M/Fabric I, Fabric P/Fabric A.

5 To assemble a block, arrange and sew together two HST units and two 2½in (6.4cm) squares into a four-patch block. Check the block is 4½in (11.4cm) square. You will need a total of thirty blocks.

6 Arrange and sew together sixteen blocks as in Fig 48. Sew this to the left side of the quilt. Set remaining blocks aside for the moment.

Fig 48

Making the Border 3B blocks

7 Using the 4½in (11.4cm) squares from Fabrics I, T, Q and U, sew sixteen squares together and sew to the right-hand side of the quilt, as in Fig 49.

Fig 49

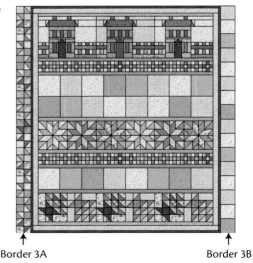

Border 3A   Border 3B

8 Arrange and sew together the remaining fifteen 4½in (11.4cm) squares into a row and sew this to the bottom of the quilt.

9 Take the remaining fourteen blocks you made for Border 3A and sew them together as in Fig 50, adding one 4½in (11.4cm) square on the right-hand side. Sew this pieced row to the top of the quilt.

Fig 50

11 Prepare the appliqué pieces (including the bird and wing) in the method of your choice. Using the photos as a guide, sew the pieces in place. Embroider the bird's tail following the template lines.

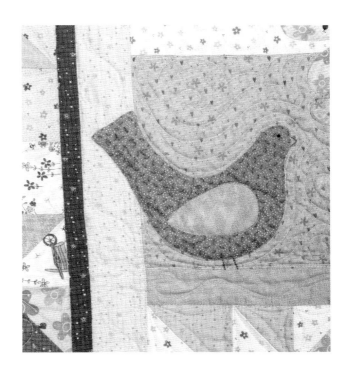

Adding the appliqués

10 For Band 3 use the templates provided to cut one bird (Fabric Y) and one wing (Fabric L). For Border 3B use the templates provided to cut five flowers (Fabric F), five flowers (Fabric J), four flowers (Fabric G), thirty-eight leaves (Fabric D), fourteen flower centres (Fabric T), stems (Fabric K) finished at ¼in (6mm) wide.

Quilt as desired. Credit for work done on this quilt goes to Wendy Sheppard for the patchwork design, Lynette Anderson for the appliqué design, Kay Harmon for the piecing and Darlene Szabo for the quilting. The pictures in the chapter show examples of the quilting, which was a mixture of machine and hand quilting. In brief, the quilting was as follows.

❈ Machine quilting in the ditch.

❈ Outline quilting around appliqué motifs.

❈ Machine quilted feather pattern in Band 2 and Band 5 (nine-patch bands).

❈ Wavy line machine quilting in the sashing strips.

❈ Curved triangles in Band 7 to emphasize the pieced triangles.

❈ Echo quilting to fill the background in Border 3B.

3 When all the quilting is finished, tidy all the thread ends, square up the quilt and prepare for binding. Cut eight strips of binding fabric, each 2½in (6.4cm) x WOF. Join the strips together using 45-degree seams. Press the seams open. Fold the strip in half all along the length, wrong sides together, and press. Use this strip to bind your quilt – see Basic Techniques: Binding. Add a label to your quilt recording your name and the date it was sewn.

Adding Border 4
12 Sew two 1in x 72½in (2.5cm x 184.2cm) Fabric S strips to the long sides of quilt. Sew two 1in x 61½in (2.5cm x 156.2cm) Fabric S strips to the top and bottom of the quilt.

Adding Border 5
13 Sew two 1½in x 73½in (3.8cm x 186.7cm) Fabric I strips to the long sides of quilt. Sew two 1½in x 63½in (3.8cm x 161.3cm) Fabric I strips to the top and bottom of the quilt.

Adding the Border 6
14 Sew two 4in x 75½in (10.2cm x 191.8cm) Fabric B strips to the sides of quilt. Sew two 4in x 70½in (10.2cm x 179cm) Fabric B strips to the top and bottom to complete the quilt top.

Quilting and finishing
1 Lay the pressed backing right side down, with the smoothed wadding (batting) on top. Lay the quilt top right side up on top, making sure there is wadding and backing showing all round, and then secure the quilt layers together (see Basic Techniques: Making a Quilt Sandwich).

Moonlight Cottage Wall Hanging

You will need...

❄ Light blue floral print for bird appliqué 4in x 5½in (10.2cm x 14cm)

❄ Light blue print for bird's wing 2in x 2½in (5cm x 6.4cm)

❄ Red heart print for heart on door 2½in x 3½in (6.4cm x 8.9cm)

❄ Light green print for front door 2½in x 6½in (6.4cm x 16.5cm)

❄ Dark brown print for lower windows 1½in x 7in (3.8cm x 17.8cm)

❄ Light brown print for upper windows 1½in x 7½in (3.8cm x 19cm)

❄ Red print for roof and chimneys 16in x 2½in (40.6cm x 6.4cm)

❄ Cream-on-cream floral print for picket fence 1½in x 27in (3.8cm x 68.6cm)

❄ Cream-on-cream stripe for picket fence and moon 2½in x 11in (6.4cm x 28cm)

❄ Blue print for sky 10½in (26.7cm) x WOF

❄ Grey print for house 3½in (8.9cm) x WOF

❄ Dark green floral print for grass 16½in x 3½in (42cm x 8.9cm)

❄ Red check fabric for outer border and binding 7½in (19cm) x WOF

❄ Valdani stranded embroidery cotton (floss): #078 aged wine (or DMC #221) and #H212 faded brown (or DMC #839)

❄ Wadding (batting) 20in (51cm) square

❄ Backing fabric 20in (51cm) square

Finished size
18in (45.7cm) square approx
Use ¼in (6mm) seams unless otherwise stated
WOF= width of fabric

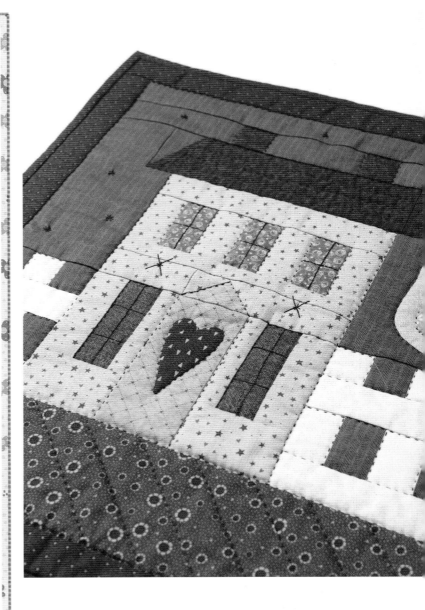

Cutting out

The house block is assembled in four sections, A, B, C and D, and the parts of each section are numbered and shown in Fig 1. As you cut the pieces for the block, label them as you go along to make them easy to find as you piece (use post-it notes). Width measurements are given first.

1 From blue print for the sky cut one strip 1½in (3.8cm) x WOF and sub-cut as follows:

❀ One strip 16½in x 1½in (42cm x 3.8cm) – A1.

❀ One rectangle 4½in x 1½in (11.4cm x 3.8cm) – A2.

❀ One rectangle 3½in x 1½in (8.9cm x 3.8cm) – A3.

❀ One rectangle 7½in x 1½in (19cm x 3.8cm) – A5.

❀ Five 1½in (3.8cm) squares – C1.

❀ Five rectangles 1½in x 2in (3.8cm x 5cm) – C4.

2 From blue print cut one strip 2½in (6.4cm) x WOF and sub-cut as follows:

❀ One 2½in (6.4cm) square – A6.

❀ One rectangle 5½in x 2½in (14cm x 6.4cm) – A10.

Using the templates provided cut one half-rectangle triangle A7 and one A8.

3 From blue print cut one strip 5in (12.7cm) x WOF and sub-cut as follows:

❀ One rectangle 5in x 3½in (12.7cm x 8.9cm) – B1.

❀ One rectangle 5in x 6½in (12.7cm x 16.5cm) – B5.

4 From red print cut the following:

❀ Two 1½in (3.8cm) squares for chimneys – A3.

❀ One rectangle 7½in x 2½in (19cm x 6.4cm) for roof – A9.

Using the templates provided cut one half-rectangle triangle A7 and one A8.

5 From grey print for house cut one strip 1½in (3.8cm) x WOF and one strip 2in x WOF. Sub-cut the 1½in (3.8cm) strip as follows:

❀ One rectangle 7½in x 1½in (19cm x 3.8cm) – B2.

❀ Four rectangles 1½in x 2½in (3.8cm x 6.4cm) – B3.

❀ Two rectangles 3½in x 1½in (8.9cm x 3.8cm) – B7.

❀ Two 1½in (3.8cm) squares (to create triangles) – B8.

❀ Two rectangles 1½in x 3½in (3.8cm x 8.9cm) – C7.

Sub-cut the 2in (5cm) strip as follows.

❀ One rectangle 7½in x 1in (19cm x 2.5cm) – B6.

❀ Two rectangles 1in x 3½in (2.5cm x 8.9cm) – C9.

❀ Two rectangles 3in x 2in (7.6cm x 5cm) – C11.

6 From light green print for door and arch, cut the following:

❀ One rectangle 2½in x 1½in (6.4cm x 3.8cm) – B9.

❀ One rectangle 2½in x 5in (6.4cm x 12.7cm) – C10.

7 From light brown print for upper windows cut three rectangles 1½in x 2½in (3.8cm x 6.4cm) – B4.

8 From dark brown print for lower windows cut two rectangles 1½in x 3½in (3.8cm x 8.9cm) – C8.

9 The picket fence uses two different cream-on-cream fabrics, but you could use just one if preferred. From cream-on-cream floral print 1½in x 27in (3.8cm x 68.6cm) cut the following:

❀ Three 1½in (3.8cm) squares – C2.

❀ Three rectangles 1½in x 2in (3.8cm x 5cm) – C5.

❀ One rectangle 3½in x 1½in (8.9cm x 3.8cm) – C3.

❀ Two rectangles 6½in x 1½in (16.5cm x 3.8cm) – C6.

10 From cream-on-cream stripe cut the following. Put aside the remainder to use for the moon appliqué later.

❀ One 1½in (3.8cm) square – C2.

❀ One rectangle 3½in x 1½in (8.9cm x 3.8cm) – C3.

❀ One rectangle 1½in x 2in (3.8cm x 5cm) – C5.

11 From red check fabric cut the following:

❀ Two 1½in x 16½in (3.8cm x 42cm) for side borders.

❀ Two 1½in x 18½in (3.8cm x 47cm) for top and bottom borders.

❀ Two 2½in (6.4cm) x WOF for binding.

Piecing the house block

12 To piece Section A, take all of the 'A' pieces and arrange them as shown in Fig 2. For the half-rectangle triangles A7 and A8, sew the triangles together along the long diagonal. Press seams towards the blue fabric. Sew the pieces together as follows.

❀ Sew pieces A2, A3, A4, A3 and A5 together into one long strip. Press seams in one direction.

❀ Sew A1 to the top of unit A2/A3/A4/A5 and press the seam upwards.

❀ Sew piece A6 to the left side of unit A7/A8. Sew A10 to the right side of the other A7/A8 unit. Sew A9 in the middle.

❀ Sew the two rows together to complete Section A.

Fig 1 House block layout
Measurements are cut sizes and include seam allowances

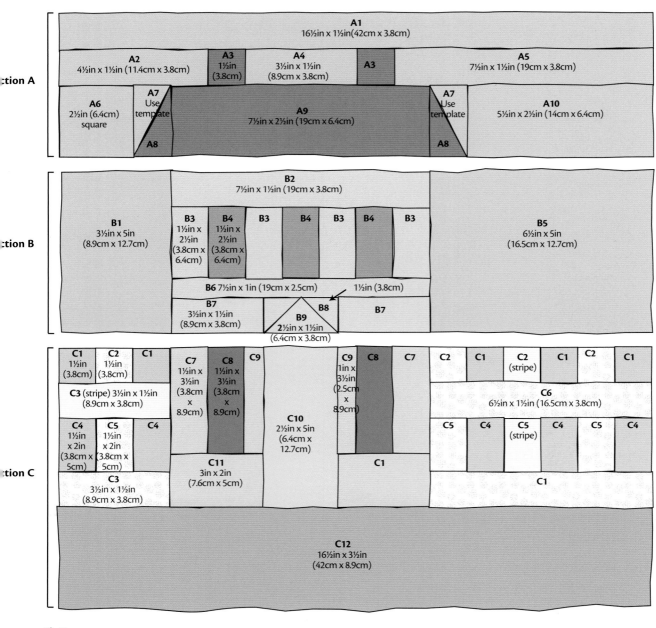

Section A

| A1 |
| 16½in x 1½in(42cm x 3.8cm) |

A2 4½in x 1½in (11.4cm x 3.8cm) | A3 1½in (3.8cm) | A4 3½in x 1½in (8.9cm x 3.8cm) | A3 | A5 7½in x 1½in (19cm x 3.8cm)

A6 2½in (6.4cm) square | A7 Use template | A9 7½in x 2½in (19cm x 6.4cm) | A8 | A7 Use template | A8 | A10 5½in x 2½in (14cm x 6.4cm)

Section B

B1 3½in x 5in (8.9cm x 12.7cm)

B2 7½in x 1½in (19cm x 3.8cm)

B3 1½in x 2½in (3.8cm x 6.4cm) | B4 1½in x 2½in (3.8cm x 6.4cm) | B3 | B4 | B3 | B4 | B3

B5 6½in x 5in (16.5cm x 12.7cm)

B6 7½in x 1in (19cm x 2.5cm) | 1½in (3.8cm)

B7 3½in x 1½in (8.9cm x 3.8cm) | B8 | B7

B9 2½in x 1½in (6.4cm x 3.8cm)

Section C

C1 1½in (3.8cm) | C2 1½in (3.8cm) | C1
C3 (stripe) 3½in x 1½in (8.9cm x 3.8cm)

C7 1½in x 3½in (3.8cm x 8.9cm) | C8 1½in x 3½in (3.8cm x 8.9cm) | C9

C9 1in x 3½in (2.5cm x 8.9cm) | C8 | C7

C2 | C1 | C2 (stripe) | C1 | C2 | C1

C4 1½in x 2in (3.8cm x 5cm) | C5 1½in x 2in (3.8cm x 5cm) | C4

C10 2½in x 5in (6.4cm x 12.7cm)

C6 6½in x 1½in (16.5cm x 3.8cm)

C3 3½in x 1½in (8.9cm x 3.8cm)

C11 3in x 2in (7.6cm x 5cm)

C1

C5 | C4 | C5 (stripe) | C4 | C5 | C4

C1

C12 16½in x 3½in (42cm x 8.9cm)

Fig 2
Piecing Section A

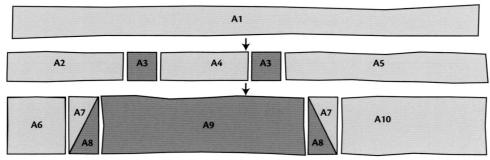

A1

A2 | A3 | A4 | A3 | A5

A6 | A7 | A9 | A7 | A10
A8 | | A8

13 To piece Section B, take all of the 'B' pieces and arrange them as shown in Fig 3. Make the B8/B9 flying geese unit as described in Basic Techniques: Making a Flying Geese Unit.

Fig 3 Piecing Section B

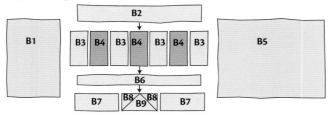

14 Now sew all the B pieces together as follows:

❀ Take the B3 and B4 rectangles and sew them together, alternating the colours as shown in Fig 3. Press the seams in one direction. Sew B2 to the top of this pieced unit.

❀ Sew one B7 to the left-hand side of a B8/B9 unit and the other B7 to the right-hand side. Press seams outwards. Sew B6 to the top of this pieced unit.

❀ Sew the units together to complete the centre section.

❀ Sew B1 to the left-hand side of the central unit and B5 to the right-hand side to complete Section B (Fig 4).

Fig 4

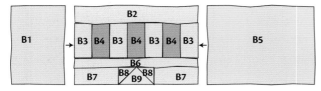

15 To piece Section C, take all of the C pieces and arrange them as shown in Fig 5. Sew the pieces together as follows:

❀ Sew a C2 cream floral square between two C1 blue squares. Sew a C3 cream stripe rectangle to the bottom of this unit. Press seams downwards. Repeat this with two C4, one C5 and one C3. Sew this unit below the top half of the unit.

❀ Sew a C8 window rectangle between C7 and C9 grey rectangles. Sew a C11 rectangle to the bottom of this unit and press seams down. Repeat this but reverse the positions of C7 and C9. Sew a C10 door rectangle between these two units.

❀ Sew a row of three blue C1 and three cream C2 squares together as Fig 5 (note that one of the squares is a cream stripe). Press seams in one direction. Repeat with three C4 and three C5 rectangles. Sew a C6 rectangle to the base of both pieced units. Now sew the units together.

❀ Sew the three pieced units together as in Fig 6. Add the C12 grass rectangle to the bottom, pressing downwards.

Fig 5 Piecing Section C

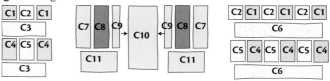

Fig 6

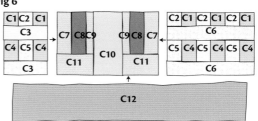

16 Finish the assembly of the block by sewing Sections A, B and C together. Press seams open. Check that the block is 16½in (42cm) square, trimming if need be.

−✕−✕−✕−✕−✕−✕−✕−✕−✕−✕−✕−✕−✕−✕−

Adding the border

17 Take the shorter red border strips and sew to the sides of the house block. Press seams outwards. Take the longer strips and sew to the top and bottom of the block and press seams outwards.

Adding the appliqué

18 For the bird and the heart appliqué use the templates provided for the Daisy Chain Cottages Quilt, (and the moon template with them). Prepare the shapes for needle-turn appliqué (see Basic Techniques: Needle-Turn Appliqué). A seam allowance of ⅛in–¼in (3mm–6mm) will be fine. Appliqué the bird in place on the right-hand fence. Using two strands of #H212 faded brown embroidery cotton (floss), embroider the bird's legs in chain stitch, the beak in satin stitch and three lines of running stitch on the tail. Add the eye with a French knot in #078 aged wine and outline the wing with running stitches. Appliqué the heart in place on the door and the moon in the sky.

19 Add further surface embroidery to the design as desired. I used two strands of #078 aged wine for the backstitch markings on the windows, and the large double cross stitches on the house front.

Quilting and finishing

20 Make a quilt sandwich of the backing fabric, wadding (batting) on top and wall hanging (see Basic Techniques: Making a Quilt Sandwich). Quilt as desired. The wall hanging was hand quilted with two strands of #078 aged wine embroidery cotton (floss) around the house, fence, bird and moon. Diagonal lines were quilted over the grass area, about 1¼in (3.2cm) apart and horizontal lines across the roof about ½in (1.3cm) apart. Finally, random stars were quilted over the sky area as small double cross stitches.

21 When all the quilting is finished, tidy all the thread ends, square up the project and prepare for binding. Join the binding strips together and press seams open. Press the strip in half along the length, right sides together. Use this double-fold strip to bind the project (see Basic Techniques: Binding).

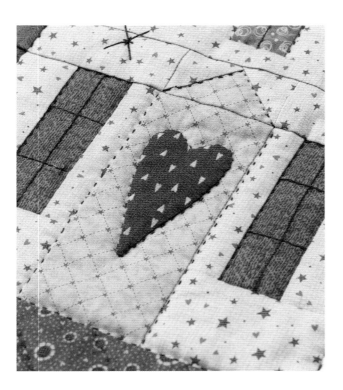

Materials & Equipment

The projects each have a list of the materials and equipment required and the basics are described here, but there's no reason why you can't experiment, especially with fabrics and embellishments.

Fabrics and wadding (batting)

For many people 100 per cent cotton fabrics are the ones of choice for patchwork and quilting but sometimes it's great to try other types of fabrics. The fabrics used to back quilts, bind quilts or to line projects such as bags can really be anything you like but cotton is the easiest to handle.

Quilt wadding (batting) is rated by its weight and is sold in standard sizes and by the yard or metre. It is available in polyester, cotton, wool and various blends and for hand and machine quilting. Thinner wadding tends to be used when machine quilting. I prefer to use Matilda's Own wool/poly blend, which is pre-washed, pre-shrunk, fully machine washable and comes in white and charcoal.

Threads

Many people like to use 100 per cent cotton thread for machine piecing and machine quilting. Polyester mixes are also popular. Threads for hand quilting can be almost anything you like. If you want the quilting to blend or tone with the fabrics then use a cotton or polyester.

For my stitcheries I mostly use Valdani, Cosmo and DMC stranded cotton (floss). These embroidery threads are in six-stranded skeins that can be split into separate strands and are available in a wide range of colours. DMC alternatives to Valdani have been provided here. Please note though that the colour matches aren't exact as Valdani threads are hand dyed.

Valdani code/colour	DMC code
#P10 antique violet	#3041
#JP122 seaside	#927
#078 aged wine	#221
#P5 tarnished gold	#712
#0511 black sea	#310
#0575 crispy leaf	#3364
#578 primitive blue	#926
#154 antique gold	#420
#H212 faded brown	#839
#031 tealish blue	#3760
#0503 garnets	#221
#512 chimney dust	#841
#514 wheat husk	#739
#0518 dusty leaves	#3781
#519 olive green	#3364
#539 evergreens	#319
#548 blackened khaki	#3031
#8103 withered mulberry	#3041

Fusible web and interfacing

Fusible web is also referred to as iron-on adhesive and is an ultra-thin sheet of adhesive backed with a special paper. When the web is placed between two fabrics, the heat of an iron causes the glue to melt and fuse the fabrics together – perfect for appliqué (see Basic Techniques: Fusible Web Appliqué). There are various makes of fusible web, including Bondaweb (also called Vliesofix or Wonder Under) and Steam-A-Seam2. Read the manufacturer's instructions before use.

Fusible interfacing works on the same principle but is single-sided. It is used to stiffen and strengthen fabrics. An iron-on stabilizer can also be used to strengthen a fabric, making it more able to support embroidery stitches. It needs to be ironed on before the stitching is started.

Buttons

I like to use buttons in my work, not just functional ones but also to represent animals' eyes, flower centres and so on. I have my own range of really cute buttons in all sorts of shapes. Some are raw wood, while others have been hand painted in Australia – see Suppliers.

Equipment

There are many tools and gadgets you could buy for patchwork and quilting but a basic tool kit is all you really need to start with.

Basic tool kit			
☑	Quilter's ruler	☑	Template plastic
☑	Rotary cutter and mat	☑	Marking pen
☑	Scissors	☑	Iron
☑	Tape measure	☑	Sewing machine
☑	Needles	☑	Embroidery hoop
☑	Pins and safety pins	☑	Fabric glue
☑	Thimble	☑	Suitable threads

Rotary cutter, ruler and mat

Patchwork is easier and quicker with a rotary cutter, mat and quilter's ruler, especially for quilt making. You will find a self-healing cutting mat 18in x 24in is very useful and a 45mm or 60mm diameter rotary cutter.

Pins and needles

You will need pins for piecing patchwork and for fastening the layers of a quilt together. Safety pins could also be used for securing the quilt sandwich. Alternatively, spray adhesives are available for this.

You will need a selection of hand sewing needles for embroidery and quilting, and machine needles for piecing and quilting. I use Clover No. 9 embroidery needles and love the smooth, quality finish the needles have. Their gold eye makes them easy to thread.

Appliqué mat

An appliqué mat is a large non-stick sheet, usually made from Teflon. One advantage to using an appliqué mat is that you can iron some of the underneath pieces in place, thus stopping them moving out of position, which allows you to place the top layers with ease. You can remove and re-position fabrics fused to an appliqué mat, but not fabrics already fused to fabrics. Keep your mat rolled up when not in use and it will last for years.

Apliquick™ tools

The revolutionary Apliquick™ tools were developed by my friend Rosa Rojas. The two rods are made from steel, which give them a nice feel in your hands as you work with them. The thicker of the rods has a forked end and this is the rod that you hold the appliqué pieces in place with. The other rod has has a bevelled edge for turning and pressing the seam allowance to the wrong side of the fabric. Both rods have a fine point on the other end, which is used when working with very small pieces.

Marking pens

In this book markers are mostly used to mark stitchery designs on to fabric. I use a fine Zig Millenium or Pigma Micron permanent marker pen, usually in brown. There are also water- and air-soluble pens that can be used to mark fabric temporarily.

Template plastic

This is a transparent plastic that can be used to create templates, which can be used many times. It is available from craft shops and patchwork and quilting suppliers. The template is traced on to the plastic and cut out with sharp scissors (don't use your fabric scissors!). Use a permanent marker to label the template.

Masking tape

This is useful to mark straight quilting lines. Simply place a long strip of the tape where you want to quilt and sew along the edge of the tape. A low-tack tape is easy to remove and doesn't leave any marks.

Appliqué paper

This comes in sheet form and is a single-sided, fusible water-soluble paper, making it ideal for use with the Apliquick™ tools or as a replacement for the traditional pre-cut papers for English paper piecing. The paper can be put through an inkjet printer, which enables you to print multiple pieces of the same shape without the need to laboriously draw them by hand. The paper does not need to be removed from the completed work, as it softens with handling and disintegrates when the finished project is washed.

Black grip mat

This mat is ideal for preventing fabrics from moving as you trace appliqué shapes and when you are working with the Apliquick™ tools. It is light and can be stored by rolling up when not in use. It can be hand washed to remove any unwanted glue residue that's left from working English paper piecing or the Apliquick method of preparing your shapes for appliqué.

Glues

There are temporary glues available that are very useful, especially for appliqué. I find Roxanne's Glue Baste-It ™ excellent as it has a fine nozzle for accurate placement of the glue. It is only a temporary glue but is handy for holding pieces in place instead of using pins. A fabric glue pen is used in the preparation of English paper pieces and in the preparation of appliqué shapes when using the Apliquick™ tools. You will also need a fast-tack craft glue for fixing the Bird Scissor Holder together. Always follow the instructions on the packet and use in a well-ventilated room.

Light box or light pad

A light box is a useful piece of equipment for tracing designs but can be expensive so try a light pad, or for no cost at all use a well-lit window. Tape the design to the light box (or pad or window), tape the fabric on top and trace the design on to the fabric. I also use a light under a glass table, which works well and stops my arms getting tired when standing at a window!

Basic Techniques

This section describes the general techniques needed to make and finish the projects in this book, from transferring designs to binding a quilt. Beginners in particular should find it very useful.

Sewing seams

Patchwork or pieced work does require that your seams are accurate in order that your blocks will fit together nicely. Maintaining an accurate ¼in (6mm) seam allowance where stated will give the best results. For really accurate piecing sew a *bare* ¼in (6mm) seam, as this will allow for the thickness of thread and the tiny amount of fabric taken up when the seam is pressed.

Pressing work

Your work will look its best if you press it well. Generally, seams are pressed towards the darker fabric to avoid dark colours showing through on the right side. If joining seams are pressed in opposite directions they will nest together nicely and create the flattest join. Press (don't iron) and be very careful with steam, as this can stretch fabric, particularly edges cut on the bias.

Using templates

The project templates are given after this section and are shown full size. Please read all of the instructions with each template carefully. Once a template is the size required you can trace it on to paper or thin card, cut it out and use it as a pattern to cut the shape from paper. Before cutting out check whether a ¼in (6mm) seam allowance is needed. If using a template for needle-turn appliqué a seam allowance will be required, but will not be needed if you are using a fusible web appliqué technique.

Templates used for fusible web appliqué will need to be reversed before use. Sometimes it is also necessary to reverse a template, so that a design will appear facing the other way. One way to reverse a template is to photocopy it and place the copy on to a light source with the template face down rather than right side up. The design is then reversed and you can trace it as normal. You could also trace the template on to tracing paper, turn the tracing paper over and trace the template again on to paper.

Transferring designs

Designs can be transferred on to fabric in various ways. I use a light source, such as a light box/pad, a window or a light under a glass table. Iron your fabric so it is free of creases. Place the design right side up and then the fabric right side up on top, taping in place if necessary. Use a fine-tipped fabric marking pen or a pencil to trace the design. If the marks might show later use a temporary marker, such as an air-erasable or water-soluble one.

Patchwork

The patchwork used in the projects is described within the relevant projects but there are two patchwork units that are used more often – half-square triangles and flying geese – and these are described here.

Making half-square triangles

Some projects use half-square triangle units, sometimes in a row or to build into larger blocks. Making two half-square triangle (HST) units at once is a quick method.

1 Take two squares, each different colours, and place them right sides together with the lighter square on top. Draw a diagonal line on the wrong side of the lighter square. Pin the squares together and stitch ¼in (6mm) either side of the drawn line (Fig 1A).

2 Cut the unit apart on the drawn line (Fig 1B) and press the seam open or towards the darker fabric (Fig 1C). Trim each unit to the correct size.

Fig 1
Making half-square triangle units

  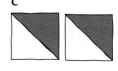

A   B   C

Making a flying geese unit

Some of the projects, such as the Little Houses Throw, use flying geese units, to build into larger blocks. One unit will need one rectangle and two smaller squares – use the sizes given in the project instructions.

1 Draw a diagonal line on the wrong side of the two smaller squares. Place one square right side together with a rectangle, aligning the left sides. Sew on the drawn line, from the centre top of the rectangle to the bottom left corner (Fig 2A). Trim ¼in (6mm) away from the sewn line to remove excess fabric and then press open to reveal the corner triangle.

2 Repeat with the other small square on the other side of the rectangle, but this time sewing from the centre top of the rectangle to the bottom right corner (Fig 2B).

Fig 2
Making a flying geese unit

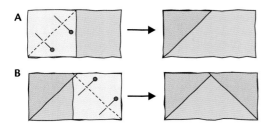

English paper piecing

This type of patchwork is also called English patchwork and uses templates, usually made of paper or thin card, which fabric pieces are wrapped around and tacked (basted) to. The patches are hand sewn together and the papers removed. Fig 3 shows the stages of a hexagon being paper pieced, Fig 4 shows a triangle and Fig 5 a star. Follow the same basic process for each of the shapes.

1 From a master template, create enough paper templates for the project. When cutting out the fabric pieces allow for a ¼in (6mm) seam all round.

2 For a hexagon follow Fig 3A–E. Pin a paper template to a fabric shape. Fold the seam allowance over the edges of the template, tacking (basting) in place through all layers. Alternatively, use a fabric glue pen. Keep the fabric firm around the paper shape and tuck in all points neatly. Repeat with all the fabric pieces.

3 Place two fabric shapes right sides together, aligning the edges, and use small whip stitches to sew together through the folded fabric but not through the paper. Place a third fabric shape right sides together with the second and sew together. Continue building the design like this. Once stitching is finished remove tacking and papers (Fig 3).

Fig 3
English paper piecing a hexagon

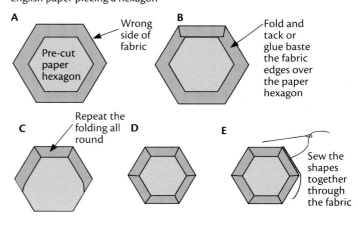

A — Wrong side of fabric
Pre-cut paper hexagon
B — Fold and tack or glue baste the fabric edges over the paper hexagon
C — Repeat the folding all round
D
E — Sew the shapes together through the fabric

Fig 4
English paper piecing a triangle

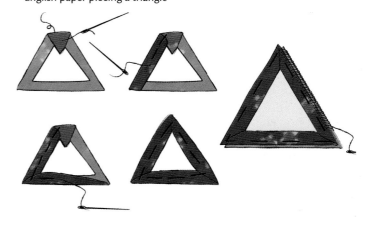

Fig 5
English paper piecing a Le Moyne Star block

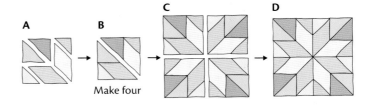

A   B   Make four   C   D

Appliqué

Appliqué is the technique of applying and fixing one fabric shape on top of another. I have used two methods – needle-turn appliqué and fusible web appliqué. You may also like to use an appliqué mat.

Needle-turn appliqué

This is a traditional method of hand appliqué where each appliqué piece has a seam turned under all round and is stitched into position on the background fabric. The appliqué shapes may be drawn freehand or templates used See also, Using Apliquick™ Tools, below.

1 Mark around the template on the wrong side of your fabric and then mark another line further out all round for the seam allowance. This is usually ¼in (6mm) but it depends on the size of the appliqué piece being stitched and type of fabric being used. Smaller pieces may only need a ⅛in (3mm) allowance. Clip into the seam allowance on concave curves (the inward ones) to make it easier to turn the seam under.

2 For each appliqué piece turn the seam allowance under all round and press. Position the appliqué on the background fabric and stitch into place with tiny slip stitches. Press when finished. Some people use the needle to turn the seam under as they stitch the appliqué in place.

Fusible web appliqué

Fusible web has an adhesive that melts with the heat of an iron, so when the web is placed between two fabrics the heat causes the fabrics to fuse together.

1 When using templates for fusible web appliqué they need to be flipped or reversed because you will be drawing the shape on the back of the fabric – see Reversing Templates. If the design is symmetrical, however, you won't need to reverse it.

2 Trace around each template on to the paper side of the fusible web, leaving about ½in (1.3cm) around each shape. Cut out roughly around each shape. Iron the fusible web, paper side up, on to the wrong side of the appliqué fabric. Now cut out accurately on your drawn line.

3 When the web is cool, peel off the backing paper and then place the appliqué in position on your project, right side up. (Check the template to see which pieces need

to go under other pieces, shown by dashed lines on the patterns.) Fuse into place with a medium-hot iron for about ten seconds. Allow to cool.

4 The edge of the appliqué can be further secured by stitches. I normally use blanket stitch as I like the hand-crafted look but machine satin stitch can also be used.

Using an appliqué mat

Using your ironing board as a work area, lay out the appliqué mat. Remove the backing paper from each appliqué piece as required and position it on the mat. Some pieces need to go beneath other pieces and these are shown by dashed lines on templates. When positioned, iron into place on the mat. Once cool, peel the whole shape from the mat, place on the background fabric and fuse with the iron.

Using Apliquick™ tools

These tools are a revolutionary way to prepare appliqué shapes and are used in conjunction with fusible water-soluble appliqué paper.

1 Begin by tracing the appliqué shapes onto the paper side of the appliqué paper. If you need to reverse the drawings, trace on the shiny/fusible side (see Photo 1).

Photo 1

2 Cut out each shape accurately on the line. Fuse the paper shiny side down on the wrong side of the fabric. Clip all concave curves to the edge of the paper, but do not clip convex curves. Cut out about ¼in (6mm) beyond the drawn line, to allow for a seam allowance (Photo 2).

Photo 2

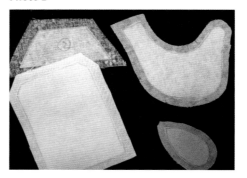

3 Place the appliqué shape face down on a flat surface. I work on a black grip mat, which prevents the shapes moving as I work. Working away from you, stroke some fabric glue onto the edge of the appliqué paper (it's ok if some glue goes on the seam allowance). I add glue in sections rather than all around the shape at once, as the glue dries into the paper fairly quickly (Photo 3).

Photo 3

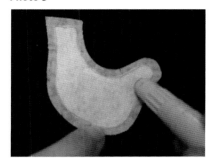

4 With the forked holding tool upright in your left hand (if right handed), rely on the weight of the tool rather than pressing down to hold the appliqué shape steady. With the bevelled-edge turning tool in your right hand and using a rolling action, slide the bevelled edge of the tool under the raw edge of the fabric and roll the seam allowance over the edge of the paper (Photo 4). Press into the glue to hold the fabric seam allowance in place. Add more glue and continue working this way until the seam allowance has been turned to the wrong side around the entire shape. Press the work (Photo 5). Sew the appliqué shape into position using a blind hem stitch and matching thread.

Photo 4

Photo 5

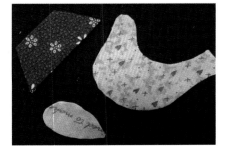

Adding a border

A border frames a quilt and can tie the whole design together. Borders can be plain and simple or pieced and I have used both types in this book. Most are sewn on with straight or butted corners.

1 Calculate the length the border should be by measuring the width of the quilt through the centre. Cut the top and bottom borders to this measurement (Fig 6A). Sew these borders to the quilt using ¼in (6mm) seams and press.

2 Measure the quilt height through the centre, including the top and bottom borders just added (Fig 6B). Cut side borders to this measurement, sew them in place and press. To add a second border, repeat steps 1 and 2.

Fig 6
Adding a border

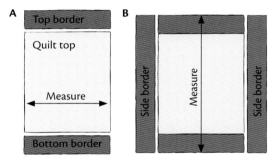

Cutting bias strips

Strips that are cut along the bias direction of a piece of fabric have more stretch than those cut on the straight grain and are therefore useful if you want fabric pieces to curve, for example in the Two Little Birds Purse project. For a quilt or project that is bound with a straight edge you don't need bias-cut strips, but you will for any project with curves.

1 Start with a square of fabric and determine which way the bias grain is running (it will be more stretchy than the other directions). Fold the square into a triangle and crease along the bias direction (Fig 7).

Fig 7
Cutting bias strips

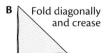

A Bias direction

 B Fold diagonally and crease

 C Open out and cut diagonal strips to desired width

2 Decide what width your bias strips need to be, place your fabric on the cutting board and, using a quilter's ruler, cut parallel strips across the fabric to this width.

Joining bias strips

When narrow strips of fabric have to be joined, particularly bias-cut strips, they are normally joined with 45-degree seams, to make the join less noticeable. Position the two strips of fabric, right sides together, at 45-degree angles as in Fig 8. Pin, sew the seam and press the seam open.

Fig 8
Joining bias strips

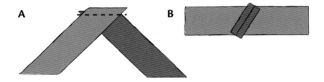

Making a quilt sandwich

A quilt sandwich is a term used to describe the three layers of a quilt – the top, the wadding (batting) and the backing. These layers need to be secured together so that a quilt will hang correctly and be free of puckers. Any hand or machine quilting you plan to do will look much better if the layers are secured well.

1 Press your backing fabric and hang out your wadding (batting) if necessary to reduce creases. Cut out your wadding and backing about 4in (10.2cm) larger all round than the quilt top. Prepare the top by cutting off or tying in stray thread ends, pressing it and sorting out seam allowances so they lay as flat as possible.

2 Lay the backing fabric right side down on a smooth surface and tape the corners to keep it flat. Put the wadding (batting) on top, smoothing out wrinkles. Now put the quilt top, right side up, on top.

3 Securing the three layers together can be done in various ways. Some people use pins or safety pins, some use tacking (basting), others use a spray glue. If using pins or tacking, use a grid pattern, spacing the lines about 3in–6in (7.6cm–15.2cm) apart. Tack the outside edges of the quilt sandwich too, about ½in (1.3cm) in from the edge. The sandwich is now ready for quilting.

Quilting

Quilting not only adds texture and interest to a quilt but also secures all the layers together. I have used a combination of hand and machine quilting on the projects in this book. The hand quilting stitch is really just a running stitch and ideally the length of the stitches and the spaces in between need to be small and even. Machine quilting has a more continuous look and the stitch length is usually about 10–12 stitches per 1in (2.5cm) and may depend on the fabric and threads you are using. How much or how little quilting you do is up to you but aim for a fairly even amount over the whole quilt. When starting and finishing hand or machine quilting, the starting knot and the thread end need to be hidden in the wadding (batting).

I have described within the projects the quilting done on the projects in this book. Some areas you might consider quilting are as follows.

❀ Quilt in the ditch (that is, in the seams between the blocks or the units that make up the blocks).

❀ Echo or contour quilt around motifs, about ¼in (6mm) out from the edge of the shape.

❀ Background quilt in a grid or cross-hatch pattern of regularly spaced lines.

❀ Motif or pattern quilt within blocks or borders by selecting a specific motif, such as a heart or flower.

Marking a quilting design

If you need to mark a quilting design on your top this can be done before or after you have made the quilt sandwich – most people do it before. There are many marking pens and pencils available but test them on scrap fabric first. If you are machine quilting, marking lines are more easily covered up. For hand quilting you might prefer to use a removable marker or a light pencil. Some water-erasable markers are set by the heat of an iron, so take care when pressing.

Binding

Binding a quilt creates a neat and secure edge all round. Binding may be single or double, with double-fold binding being more durable and probably best for bed quilts.

1 Measure your quilt top around all the edges and add about 10in (25.5cm) extra – this is the length of binding you need. Cut 2½in (6.4cm) wide strips (or 2¼in/5.7cm if you prefer) and join them all together to make the length needed. Fold the binding in half along the length, wrong sides together, and press.

2 Start midway along one side of the quilt and pin the binding along the edge, aligning the raw edges. Start stitching about 6in (15.2cm) away from the end of the binding and stitch through all layers using a ¼in (6mm) seam. When you reach a corner stop ¼in (6mm) away from the end (see Fig 9A).

Fig 9
Binding
A

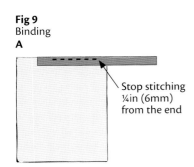

Stop stitching ¼in (6mm) from the end

3 Remove the work from the machine and fold the binding up, northwards, so it is aligned straight with the edge of the quilt, creating a mitred corner (Fig 9B).

B

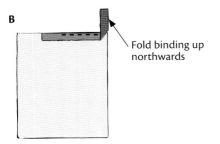

Fold binding up northwards

4 Hold the corner and fold the binding back down, southwards, aligning it with the raw edge and with the folded corner square. Pin in position and then begin sewing again, from the top and over the fold, continuing down to the next edge (Fig 9C). Repeat this folding process on the other corners.

C

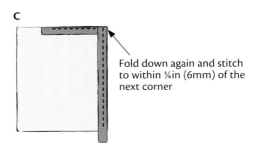

Fold down again and stitch to within ¼in (6mm) of the next corner

5 When you are nearing the starting point stop about 6in (15.2cm) away. Fold back the beginning and end of the binding, so they touch and mark these folds with a pin. Cut the binding ¼in (6mm) away from the pin, open out the binding and join the ends together with a ¼in (6mm) seam. Press the seam open, re-fold and press the binding and then slipstitch in place.

6 Fold the binding over to the back of the quilt and slipstitch it in place all round. Fold the mitres at the corners neatly and secure with tiny slipstitches. Press the sewn binding all round to finish.

Labelling your quilt

When you have finished your quilt it is important to label it, even if the information you record is just your name and the date the quilt was made. When looking at antique quilts it is always interesting to piece together information about the quilt, so you can be sure that any extra information you put on your label will be of immense interest to quilters of the future. A very simple method of labelling is to write on a piece of calico with a permanent marker pen and then appliqué this to the back of your quilt.

Embroidery stitches

I have used various stitches to create the stitcheries on the projects in this book. They are all easy to work and fun to do. Follow these simple diagrams.

Blanket stitch

Blanket stitch can be used to edge appliqué motifs and can also be stitched in a circle for flowers. This is my version of this stitch. The conventional method often allows the thread to slip under the edges of the appliqué, allowing raw edges to be seen and this method avoids that.

Start at the edge of the appliqué shape, taking the needle through to the back of the work and come back through to the front of the shape that you are appliquéing, a small distance in from the edge where you started. Pull the thread through to form a loop. Put your needle through the loop from front to back, making sure the loop is not twisted. As you pull the thread into place lift the stitch slightly so that it sits on top of the raw edge rather than sliding underneath. Pull the thread firmly into place to avoid loose, floppy stitches. Continue on to make the next stitch.

A

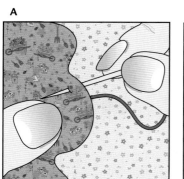

B

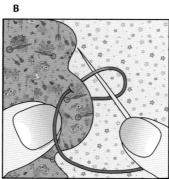

C

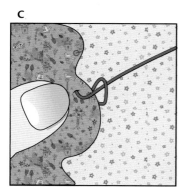

D

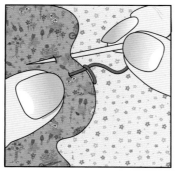

Backstitch

Backstitch is an outlining stitch that I also use to 'draw' parts of a design. It is really easy to work and can follow any parts of a design you choose.

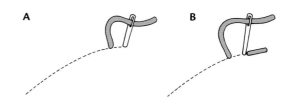

Chain stitch

This stitch can be worked in straight or curved lines and also as a detached stitch. I like using it for flower and leaves.

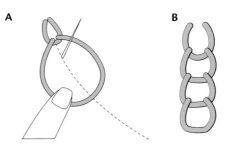

Cross stitch

A simple cross stitch is used in many of the stitcheries to add pattern or to outline part of a design.

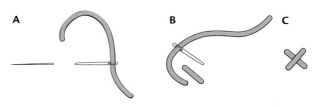

French knot

These little knots are easy to form and are useful for eyes and other details.

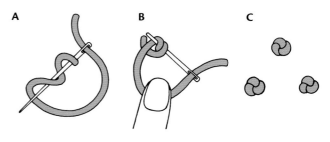

Herringbone stitch

This stitch can be used to outline areas or form patterns. It was used to stitch the Bird Scissor Holder together.

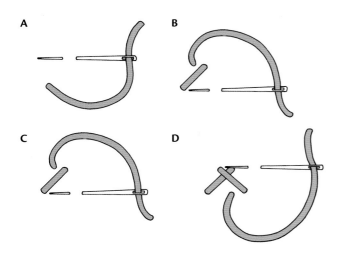

Long stitch

Long stitch is just that, a single long stitch. It is useful for coat markings, animal whiskers, flower parts and so on.

Lazy daisy stitch

This decorative stitch is great for flowers, especially if the stitches are worked in a circle.

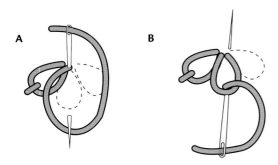

Running stitch

A running stitch is a line of evenly spaced stitches that can run in any direction or pattern you choose. Quilting stitch is a running stitch.

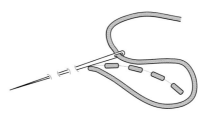

Satin stitch

This stitch is used to fill in areas of a design, with long stitches worked smoothly side by side.

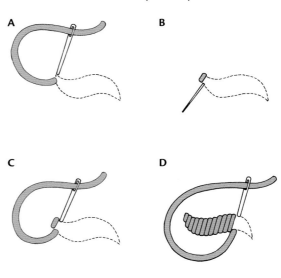

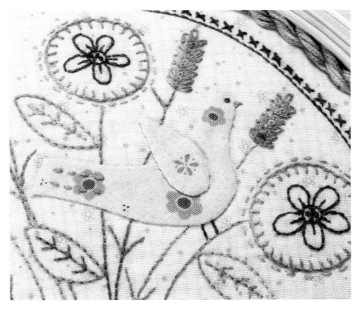

Templates

This section contains the stitchery and appliqué templates for the projects. The templates are all full size. A 1in square is shown on the pages to indicate scale. Please read the instructions with each template carefully. Some templates need to have seam allowances added and this is marked. See also Basic Techniques for Using Templates and Transferring Designs.

Hexi Birds

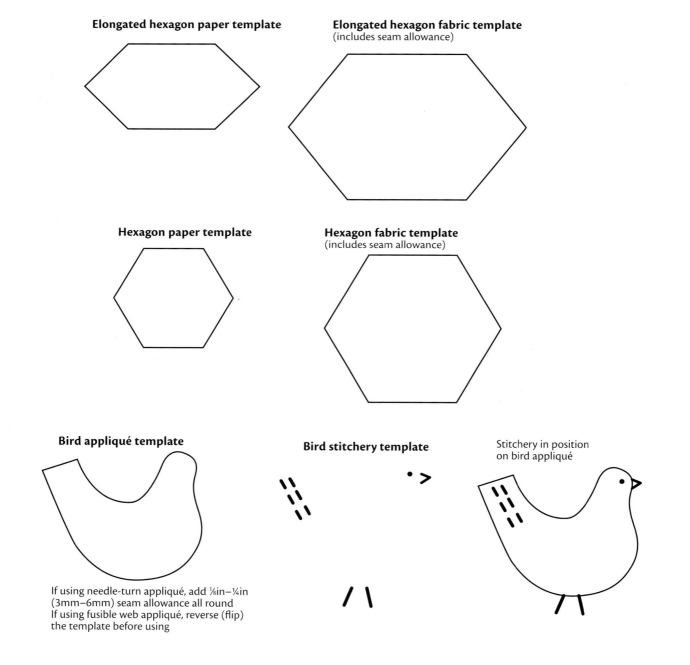

Elongated hexagon paper template

Elongated hexagon fabric template
(includes seam allowance)

Hexagon paper template

Hexagon fabric template
(includes seam allowance)

Bird appliqué template

If using needle-turn appliqué, add ⅛in–¼in (3mm–6mm) seam allowance all round
If using fusible web appliqué, reverse (flip) the template before using

Bird stitchery template

Stitchery in position on bird appliqué

Flower Sewing Basket

Templates for stitchery and appliqué

Red lines show appliqué placement
Black lines show the stitchery lines
Green lines show surface stitchery
on top of appliqué

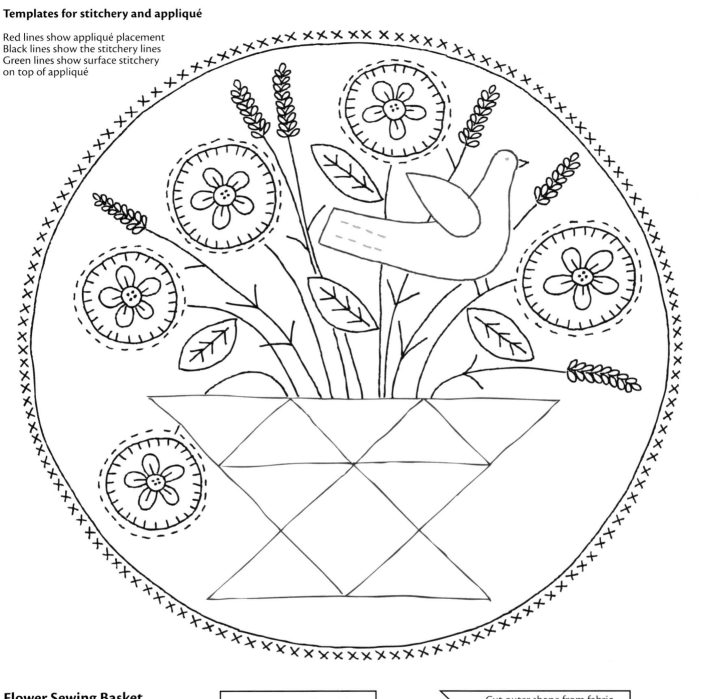

Flower Sewing Basket

Templates for English paper piecing

1 inch square

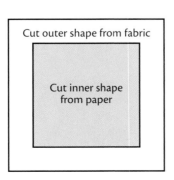

Cut outer shape from fabric

Cut inner shape
from paper

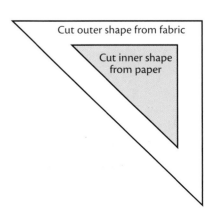

Cut outer shape from fabric

Cut inner shape
from paper

Bird Scissor Holder

Template for stitchery and appliqué

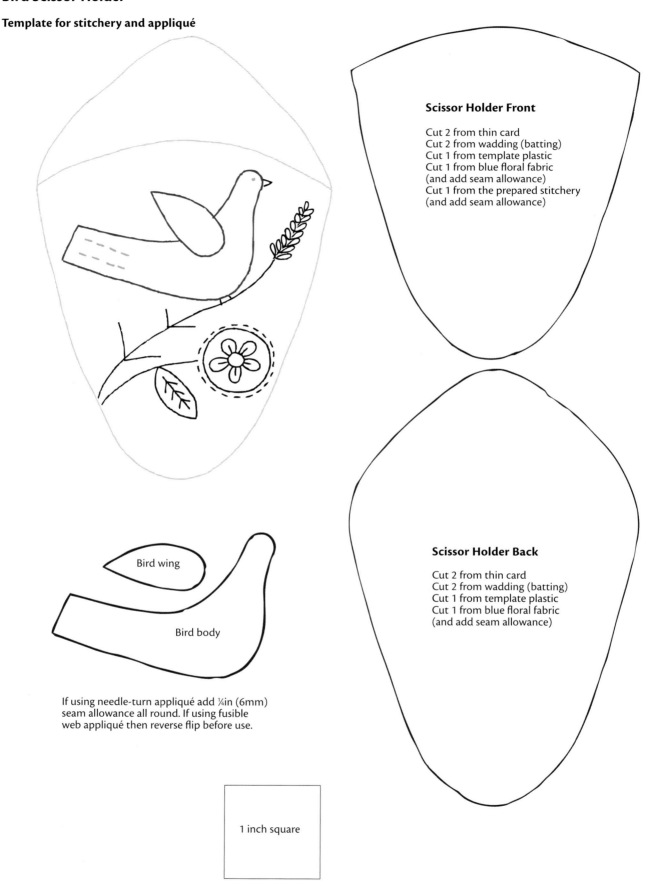

Bird wing

Bird body

If using needle-turn appliqué add ¼in (6mm) seam allowance all round. If using fusible web appliqué then reverse flip before use.

Scissor Holder Front

Cut 2 from thin card
Cut 2 from wadding (batting)
Cut 1 from template plastic
Cut 1 from blue floral fabric
(and add seam allowance)
Cut 1 from the prepared stitchery
(and add seam allowance)

Scissor Holder Back

Cut 2 from thin card
Cut 2 from wadding (batting)
Cut 1 from template plastic
Cut 1 from blue floral fabric
(and add seam allowance)

1 inch square

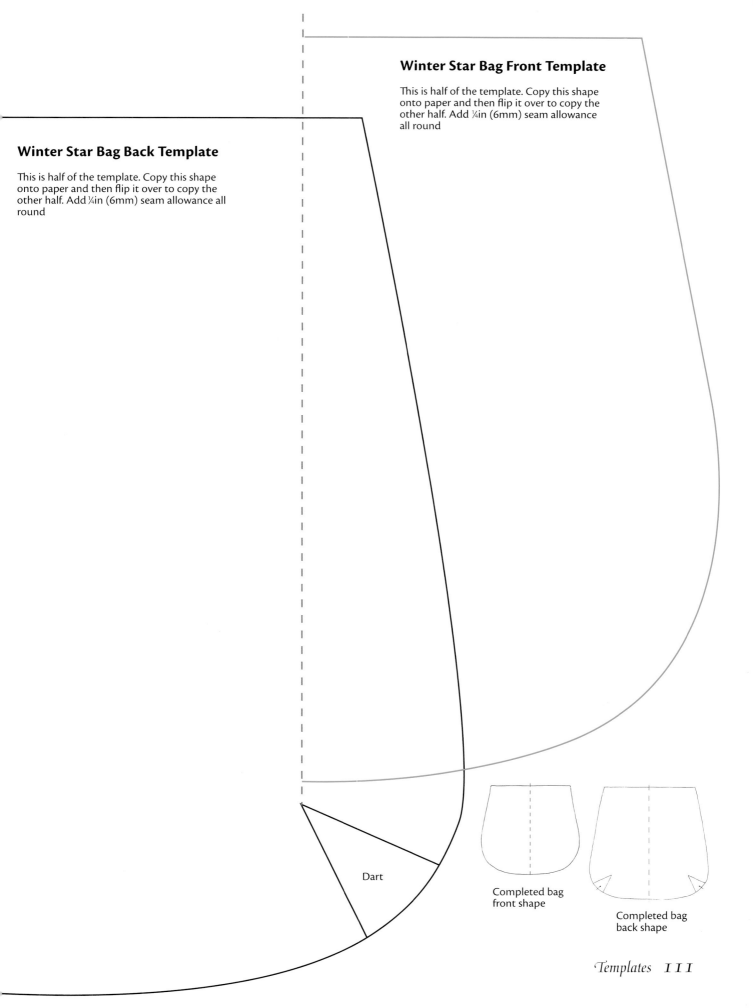

Winter Star Bag Front Template

This is half of the template. Copy this shape onto paper and then flip it over to copy the other half. Add ¼in (6mm) seam allowance all round

Winter Star Bag Back Template

This is half of the template. Copy this shape onto paper and then flip it over to copy the other half. Add ¼in (6mm) seam allowance all round

Dart

Completed bag front shape

Completed bag back shape

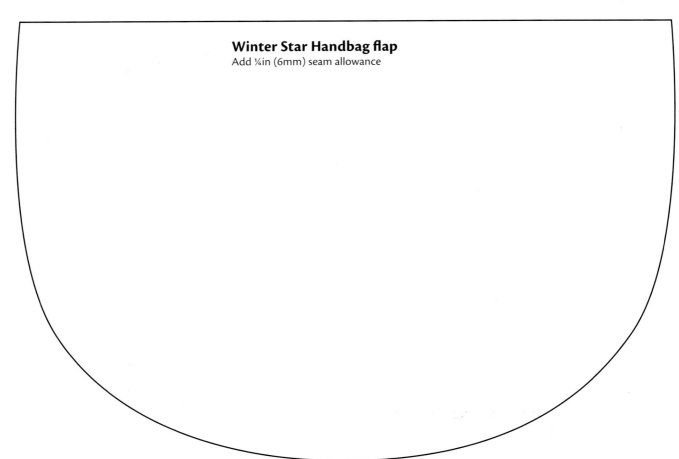

Winter Star Handbag flap
Add ¼in (6mm) seam allowance

Winter Star Handbag
Stitchery and appliqué template Winter Stars Handbag

Red lines show appliqué placement
Black lines show the stitchery lines
Green lines show surface stitchery on top of appliqué

Flap circle stitchery

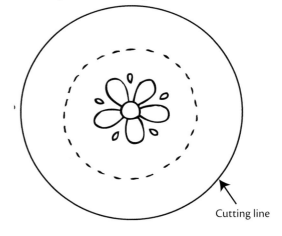

Cutting line

Eight-Point Star block template
Copy the shapes on to the template plastic. Use the plastic templates to cut out the plastic pieces, adding ¼ (6mm) all round for a seam allowance.

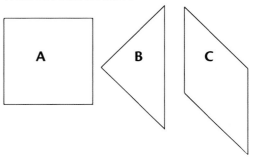

Little Houses

Appliqué templates

1in square
for scale

Stitchery pattern

Dashed lines indicate an area that will be under another piece of appliqué
If using needle-turn appliqué add ¼in (6mm) all round
If using fusible web appliqué, reverse the templates before use

Red lines indicate appliqué placement
Black lines indicate stitchery lines
Green lines indicate surface stitchery

Friends Table Topper

Hexagon fabric template
Seam allowance is included

Equilateral triangle paper template (if not using pre-cut shapes)

Hexagon paper template

Stitchery template
Use this for the coaster too

Outer triangle paper template (or you could cut down pre-cut hexagons)

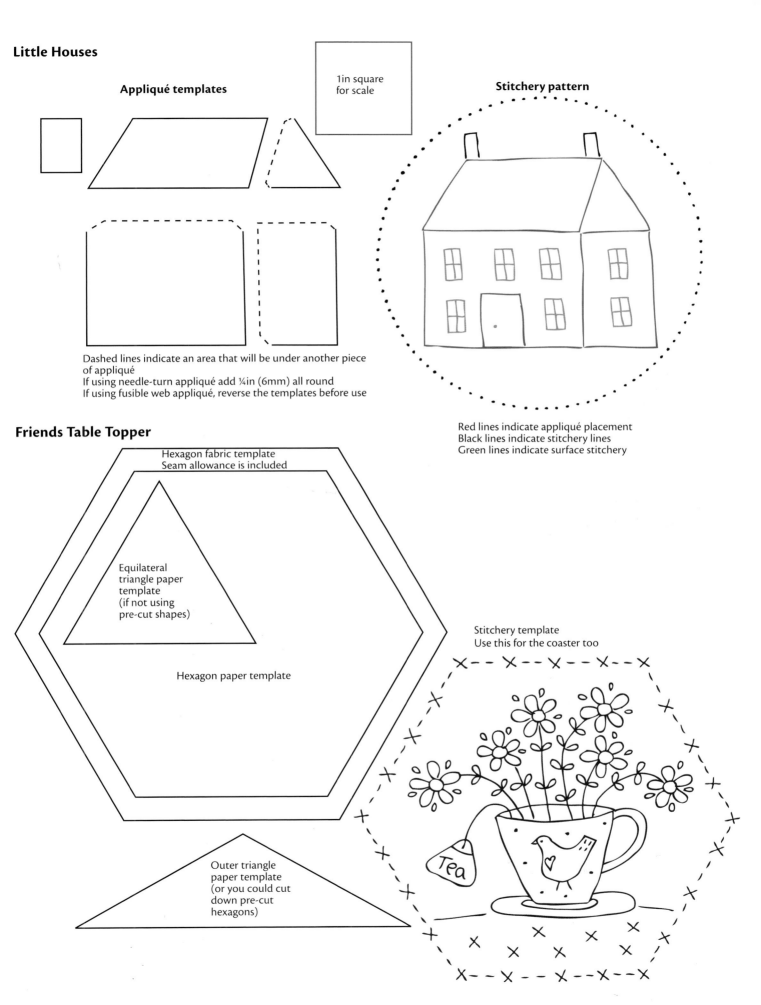

Tea

Teatime Coasters

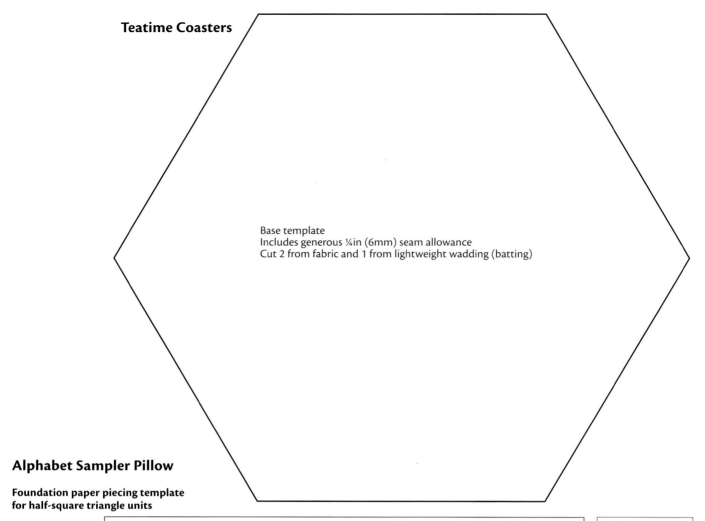

Base template
Includes generous ¼in (6mm) seam allowance
Cut 2 from fabric and 1 from lightweight wadding (batting)

Alphabet Sampler Pillow

**Foundation paper piecing template
for half-square triangle units**

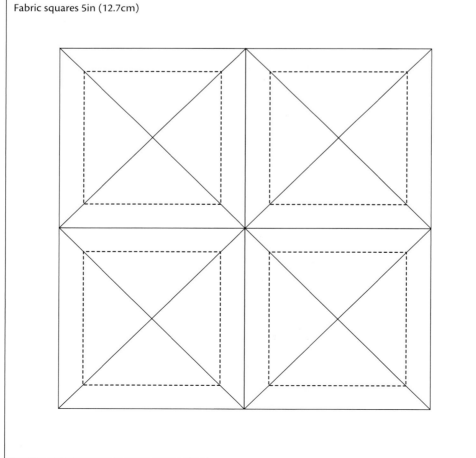

Fabric squares 5in (12.7cm)

1in square
for scale

Place two different 5in (12.7cm) squares of fabric right sides together. Place the paper template on top and pin in place. Sew along the dashed lines around each square, using a short stitch length (1.5mm). Cut the units apart on all the solid lines (vertical, horizontal and diagonal). Press seams away from the paper and then on the wrong side fold the paper on the stitched seam and gently tear the paper away at an angle, from both sides of the stitched line.

Alphabet Sampler Pillow

Appliqué and stitchery templates

Stitchery pattern   Red lines indicate appliqué placement
Black lines indicate stitchery lines
Green lines indicate surface stitchery

Appliqué templates
If using needle-turn appliqué add ¼in (6mm) all round
If using fusible web appliqué, reverse the templates
before use

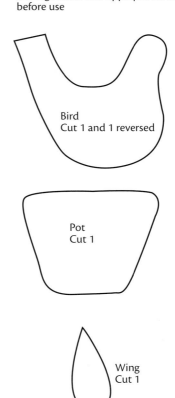

Bird
Cut 1 and 1 reversed

Pot
Cut 1

Wing
Cut 1

Heart Mini Cushion

Red lines indicate appliqué placement
Black lines indicate stitchery lines
Green lines indicate surface stitchery

Stitchery pattern

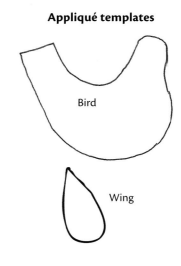

Appliqué templates

Bird

Wing

1in square
for scale

Daisy Chain Cottages Quilt

Templates for Band 1 (Houses)

Templates for house half-rectangle units

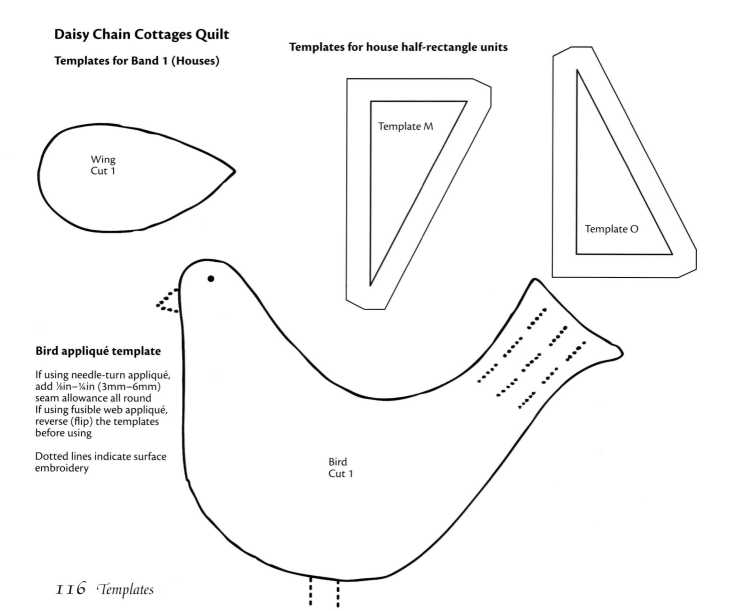

Wing
Cut 1

Template M

Template O

Bird appliqué template

If using needle-turn appliqué,
add ⅛in–¼in (3mm–6mm)
seam allowance all round
If using fusible web appliqué,
reverse (flip) the templates
before using

Dotted lines indicate surface
embroidery

Bird
Cut 1

Two Little Birds Purse

Templates

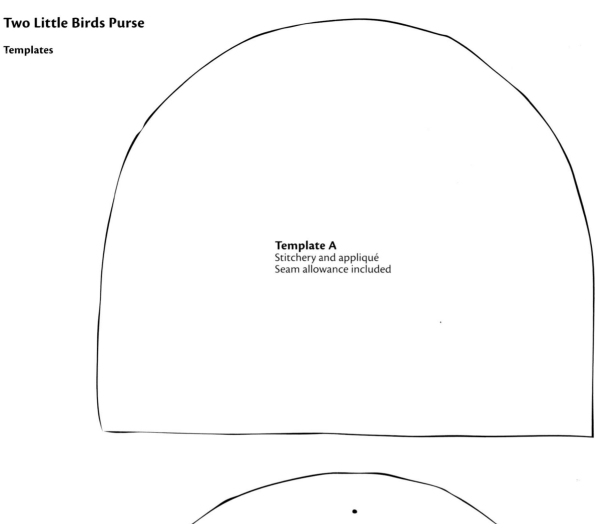

Template A
Stitchery and appliqué
Seam allowance included

Template B
Seam allowance included

Red lines show appliqué placement
Black lines show the stitchery lines
Green lines show surface stitchery on
top of appliqué

Daisy Chain Cottages Quilt

Templates for Band 3
(Four-Patch and Appliqué)

The wheelbarrow appliqué is shown full size in two sections. Copy the sections and join them at the dashed lines

If using needle-turn appliqué, add ⅛in–¼in (3mm–6mm) seam allowance all round
If using fusible web appliqué, reverse (flip) the template before using

———————	Tracing line
– – – – –	Tracing line will be under other fabrics
· · · · · · · · ·	Embroider these features

Daisy Chain Cottages Quilt

Templates for Band 3 (Four-Patch and Appliqué)

If using needle-turn appliqué, add
⅛in–¼in (3mm–6mm) seam allowance all round
If using fusible web appliqué, reverse (flip)
the templates before using

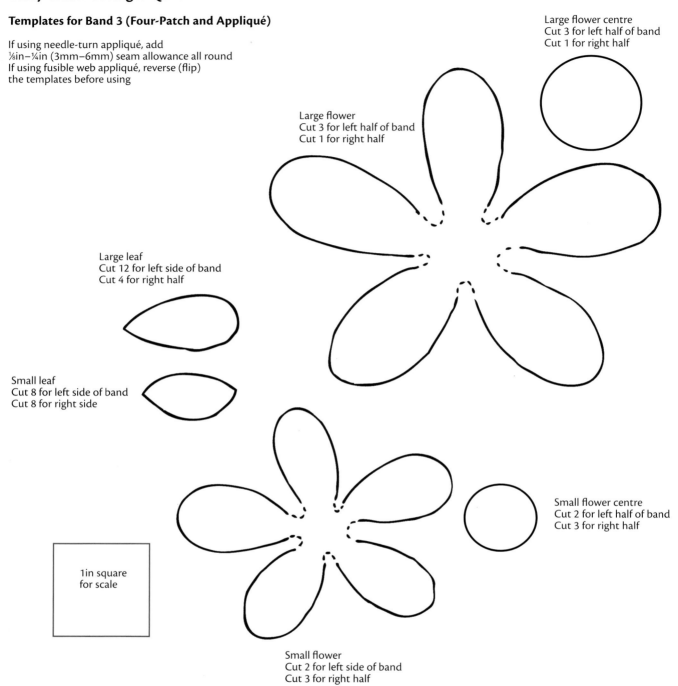

Large flower centre
Cut 3 for left half of band
Cut 1 for right half

Large flower
Cut 3 for left half of band
Cut 1 for right half

Large leaf
Cut 12 for left side of band
Cut 4 for right half

Small leaf
Cut 8 for left side of band
Cut 8 for right side

Small flower centre
Cut 2 for left half of band
Cut 3 for right half

1in square
for scale

Small flower
Cut 2 for left side of band
Cut 3 for right half

Daisy Chain Cottages Quilt

Templates for Band 4 (Le Moyne Star)

Use English paper piecing to prepare and piece for the star blocks

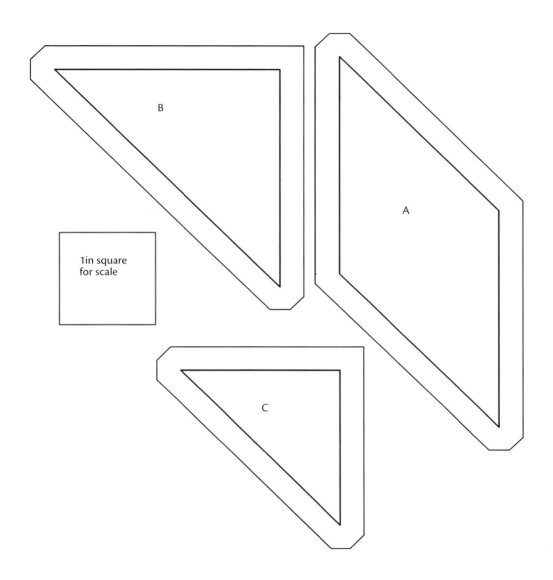

B

A

1in square
for scale

C

Daisy Chain Cottages Quilt

Templates for Band 6 (Appliqué squares)

Cut two of each shape

If using needle-turn appliqué, add ⅛in–¼in (3mm–6mm) seam allowance all round

If using fusible web appliqué, reverse (flip) the templates before using

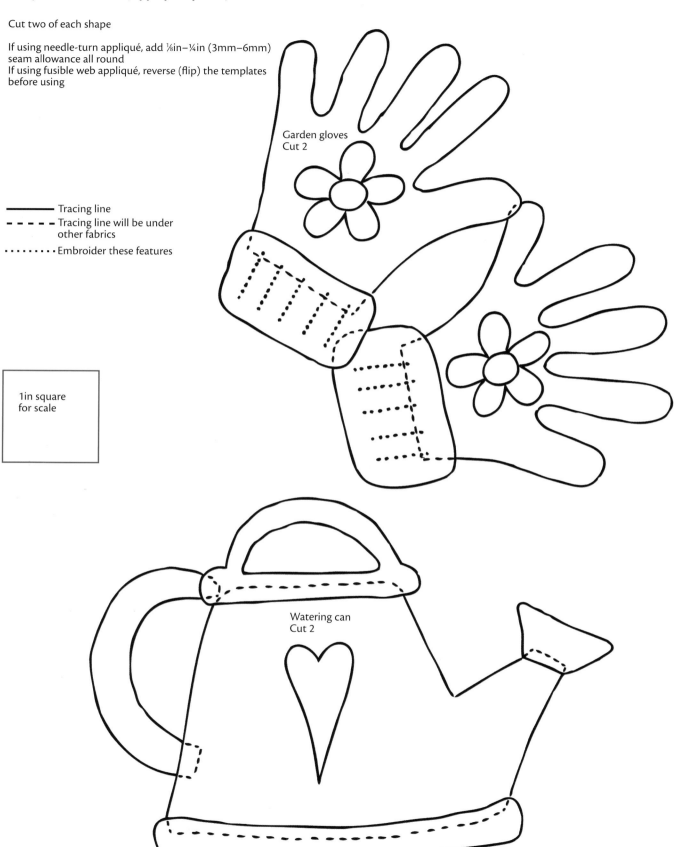

─────── Tracing line

– – – – – Tracing line will be under other fabrics

· · · · · · · Embroider these features

1in square for scale

Garden gloves
Cut 2

Watering can
Cut 2

Daisy Chain Cottages Quilt

Templates for Band 6 (Appliqué squares)

Cut two of each shape

If using needle-turn appliqué, add ⅛in–¼in (3mm–6mm)
seam allowance all round
If using fusible web appliqué, reverse (flip) the templates
before using

———————— Tracing line
– – – – – Tracing line will be under other fabrics
· · · · · · · · Embroider these features

Flower
Cut 2

Flower centre
Cut 2

Flower in pot
Cut 2

Daisy Chain Cottages Quilt

Templates for Border 3B and bird on Band 3

If using needle-turn appliqué, add ⅛in–¼in (3mm–6mm) seam allowance all round
If using fusible web appliqué, reverse (flip) the templates before using

Border 3B appliqué

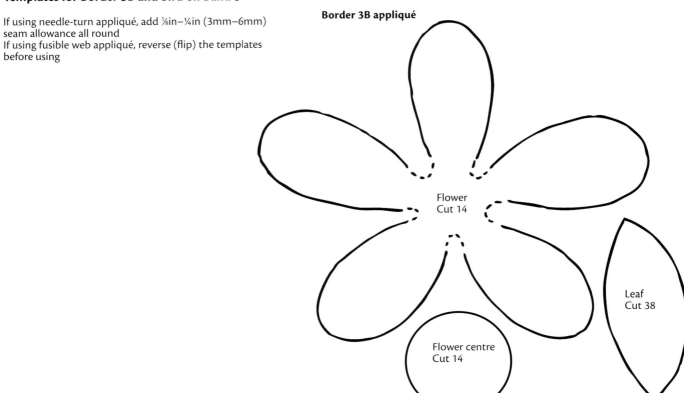

Flower
Cut 14

Leaf
Cut 38

Flower centre
Cut 14

Band 3 bird appliqué

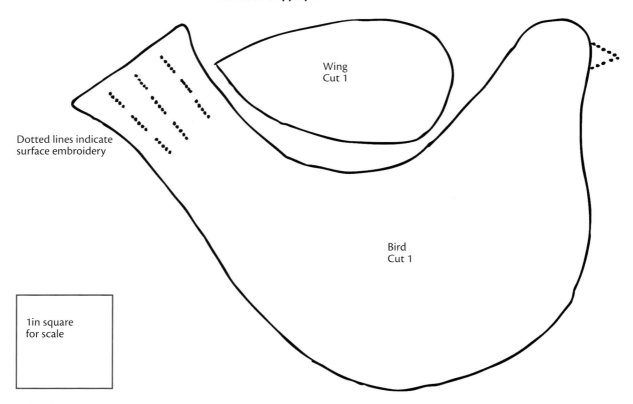

Wing
Cut 1

Dotted lines indicate
surface embroidery

Bird
Cut 1

1in square
for scale

Suppliers

Australia

Little Quilt Store

924 David Low Way, Marcoola, Sunshine Coast,
QLD 4564 Australia
Tel: +61 (7) 5450 7497
Email: sales@littlequiltstore.com.au
www.littlequiltstore.com.au
*For Lynette's books, fabrics, buttons, kits, Apliquick™
tools, appliqué paper, wooden frames, English paper
pieces, Valdani and Cosmo threads, wire quilt hangers,
zips, plastic domes, bag parts and straps*

Lynette Anderson Designs

PO Box 9314, Pacific Paradise, QLD 4564, Australia
Tel: +61 (7) 5450 7497
Email: info@lynetteandersondesigns.com.au
www.lynetteandersondesigns.com.au
*For pattern and button wholesale enquires and
teaching information*

UK & Europe

Patchwork Chicks

75b Gisburn Road, Nelson, Lancashire BB9 6DX, UK
Tel: +44 1282 619759
www.patchworkchicks.com

Cross Patch

Blaen Bran Farm, Velindre, Llandysul,
Carmarthenshire SA44 5XT, UK
Tel: +44 01559 371018
Email: enquiries@cross-patch.co.uk

Stitch Craft Create

www.stitchcraftcreate.co.uk
*Crafters' heaven! Here you'll find a large selection of
crafty products, from fabrics and wools (yarns) to craft
books and patterns. There's also a wonderful section
filled with ideas and free projects.*

USA

Sew Graceful Quilting

14094 Pleasant Ridge Road, Rogers, AR 72756, USA
Tel: +1 479-372-7403
www.sewgracefulquilting.com

RJR Fabrics

2610 Columbia Street, B, Torrance, CA 90503
Tel: (800) 422-5426
(310) 222-8782
Fax: (310) 222-8792
Email: info@rjrfabrics.com
www.rjrfabrics.com
For wholesale fabric enquiries

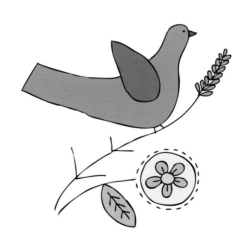

About the Author

Lynette Anderson has cultivated a worldwide following unparalleled by any other designer in the quilting industry. Whether you are a lover of embellishing, stitchery, patchwork design, quilting fabric, or a bit of everything rolled into one, Lynette offers a complete package. From her rural upbringing in Dorset, England, Lynette has always loved country life. She learned sewing, knitting, embroidery and painting at a very early age under the instruction of her mother, Ruth, and both her grandmothers. She stumbled into the craft of quilt making while searching for a creative outlet when her three boys were small. Her interest soon grew into a thriving career in teaching and pattern designing, and eventually to the launch of her own business, Lynette Anderson Designs, which she continued to grow after migrating with her family to Australia in 1990.

Since 1995, Lynette has published nine books, countless patterns, stitchery designs, handcrafted wooden buttons and fifteen quilting fabric ranges, making Lynette Anderson Designs one of the most successful businesses in the quilt cottage industry. Lynette's designs are as vast as her imagination and always incorporate a touch of whimsy. Her sophisticated folk-art design style is distinctive. Her unique blend of simple stitchery, appliqué and piecing in quilt design has struck a chord with embroiderers and quilters all over the world.

She begins the design process with hand drawings, which are then transferred to computer to be finalized. The inspiration for her patterns and fabrics come from childhood adventures and evening walks with her husband, Vince and dog Hugo in the rainforest near their current home. From a memory or a chance encounter, Lynette first draws out her ideas, often without an end product in mind. Sometimes a quilt will start with an idea for just one block. 'I have always loved textiles. The feel and the smell of new fabrics, combined with inspirational colour combinations make my heart smile.'

These days Lynette splits her time, working and designing from her home or her nearby studio and shop, which she aptly named 'Little Quilt Store', nestled along the beautiful Sunshine Coast in Queensland, Australia. Lynette enjoys travelling and lecturing around the world in the US, Japan, Canada and throughout Europe. For more information visit www. lynetteandersondesigns.com.au or follow her blog at www.lynetteandersondesigns.typepad.com

Acknowledgments

There are always so many people to thank when you are writing a book, as it is such a team effort. I give my heartfelt thanks to the many wonderful ladies that have become my friends, without whom I could not have created and stitched the gorgeous projects for this book. Thanks to Yvonne Dann – your stitching is superb and I treasure both your friendship and your willingness to stitch yet another project for me. Much gratitude to Anne, Monica, Roslyn and Beverley for their wonderful stitching help, and to Pam Grant for her hand quilting on the gorgeous Hexie Birds quilt. Thanks to Wendy Sheppard, for her patience with me and her amazing maths skills on the pieced part of the Daisy Chain Cottages Quilt. Grateful thanks to Kay Harmon, my good friend, who does lovely piecing and even lovelier appliqué, and to her friend Darlene Szabo for her wonderful machine quilting.

A special thank you to my editor Lin Clements, without whom many important details on how to make the projects would have been forgotten. My deep appreciation also goes to the whole team at David & Charles for producing yet another gorgeous book. I am truly blessed to have all these people in my life, who give their time to me with such happy hearts. Thank you all.

Index

A DAVID & CHARLES BOOK
© F&W Media International, Ltd 2015

David & Charles is an imprint of F&W Media International, Ltd
Brunel House, Forde Close, Newton Abbot, TQ12 4PU, UK

F&W Media International, Ltd is a subsidiary of F+W Media, Inc
10151 Carver Road, Suite #200, Blue Ash, OH 45242, USA

Text and Designs © Lynette Anderson 2015
Layout and Photography © F&W Media International, Ltd 2015

First published in the UK and USA in 2015

A catalogue record for this book is available from the British Library.

ISBN-13: 978-1-4463-0595-9 paperback
ISBN-10: 14463-0595-3 paperback

ISBN-13: 978-1-4463-7174-9 PDF
ISBN-10: 1-4463-7174-3 PDF

ISBN-13: 978-1-4463-7173-2 EPUB
ISBN-10: 1-4463-7173-5 EPUB

Printed in China by RR Donnelley for:
F&W Media International, Ltd
Brunel House, Forde Close, Newton Abbot, TQ12 4PU, UK

10 9 8 7 6 5 4 3 2 1

Acquisitions Editor: Sarah Callard
Managing Editor: Honor Head
Project Editor: Linda Clements
Designer: Mia Farrant
Photographer: Jason Jenkins
Production Manager: Beverley Richardson

F+W Media publishes high quality books on a wide range of subjects.
For more great book ideas visit: www.stitchcraftcreate.co.uk
Layout of the digital edition of this book may vary depending on reader hardware and display settings.